"After more than fifty years living as a
gratitude is the key to contentment. It
Practicing Thankfulness. This remarkable work provides thorough biblical support as
to how God-focused gratitude alters a Christian's orientation to himself, to others,
and ultimately to the Lord himself. The pages are filled with practical guidelines
to help a believer seize every life situation as a powerful opportunity to cultivate
a glad and thankful heart. I give *Practicing Thankfulness* a double thumbs-up!"

Joni Eareckson Tada, Founder and CEO, Joni and Friends International
Disability Center; author, *Joni*; *A Place of Healing*; and *When God Weeps*

"Christians have much to be thankful for—more than we could possibly imagine.
But *knowing* we should be thankful isn't the same thing as *living* a life marked by
thankfulness and gratitude. Sam Crabtree provides a helpful and essential book that
reminds Christians of what we have received in Christ and in the gospel as well as
practical steps to cultivate a thankful heart. We should be thankful for this book."

R. Albert Mohler Jr., President, The Southern Baptist Theological Seminary

"As I read *Practicing Thankfulness*, I was freshly inspired by the beauty, necessity,
and power of a grateful lifestyle and found myself thinking, *Every believer needs to
read this book.* Not long ago, my precious husband, Robert, and I were plunged
into turbulent waters as he was faced with two back-to-back cancer diagnoses
(during a pandemic). Through it all, even in the midst of the most difficult days,
gratitude has been a life preserver for our hearts, has transformed our perspective,
and has infused us with unexplainable peace and joy. This terrific book will show
you how thankfulness can do the same for you."

Nancy DeMoss Wolgemuth, author; Founder, Revive Our Hearts and
True Woman

"What a spiritually refreshing book this is! Reasoning from dozens of passages of Scripture, and showing substantial theological insight, Sam Crabtree explains blessing after
blessing that come from a heart filled with continual thanksgiving, even in hardship.
This is the best treatment of thanksgiving I have ever read. Highly recommended!"

Wayne Grudem, Distinguished Research Professor of Theology and
Biblical Studies, Phoenix Seminary

"With theological precision and pastoral wisdom, Sam Crabtree helps us understand
why it matters that our hearts are overflowing with thankfulness to God and how
we can cultivate this godly grace in our lives. For many of us, this will be the most
important book we read this year."

Bob Lepine, Cohost, *FamilyLife Today*; Teaching Pastor, Redeemer
Community Church, Little Rock, Arkansas

"In the midst of uncertain days we take comfort in the certainty of Christ's love for us. We have so much to be thankful for! Many of us are asking along with the psalmist: 'What shall I render to the LORD for all his benefits to me?' The answer to this question is authoritatively inscribed in Psalm 116 and beautifully illustrated here in *Practicing Thankfulness*. Powerful and practical, this book is an invitation to come and see and enjoy what the Lord has done, lifting up the cup of salvation in response."

Gloria Furman, author, *Alive in Him* and *Labor with Hope*

"An attitude of gratitude is always in season. And I want to be around anyone who reminds me of this. Sam Crabtree is that guy. In this book, he has given us a well-crafted, engaging, thoughtful, and, most importantly, biblical look into thanksgiving (not the holiday, but the Christian virtue and lifestyle). He reminds us that God is great, and so we worship him. God is good, and so we give thanks. Amen! Not many books are solely designed to encourage thankfulness. This is one, and thus deserves your attention and a place on your bookshelf. But before you put it there, read it. It will remind you of the importance of giving thanks to God for everything, beginning with this book."

Anthony J. Carter, Lead Pastor, East Point Church, East Point, Georgia

"Giving thanks is not theoretical for Sam Crabtree. He knows it. He lives it. And now he's studied it and labored to put one of his life's works into these pages for you to enjoy. Those of us who have long known Sam and labored with him in pastoral ministry have seen the message of this book in action. And now we get to go behind the curtain and see more of what makes Sam such an example of Christian gratitude. Neither he nor his fellow pastors will pretend that he's a perfect example, but in a day in which so many seem to be sinking deeper and deeper into cynicism and ingratitude, Sam is a genuine model and gifted teacher of giving thanks."

David Mathis, Senior Teacher and Executive Editor, desiringGod.org; Pastor, Cities Church, Saint Paul, Minnesota; author, *Habits of Grace*

"I thank God for Sam Crabtree. He is a wise and jovial brother who practices what he preaches in this book: he gives thanks in all circumstances. (Don't miss the last chapter—a creative list of one hundred practical ways to be thankful.)"

Andy Naselli, Associate Professor of Systematic Theology and New Testament, Bethlehem College & Seminary; Pastor, Bethlehem Baptist Church, Minneapolis

PRACTICING
THANKFULNESS

PRACTICING THANKFULNESS

CULTIVATING A GRATEFUL HEART IN ALL CIRCUMSTANCES

SAM CRABTREE

CROSSWAY®

WHEATON, ILLINOIS

Practicing Thankfulness: Cultivating a Grateful Heart in All Circumstances

Copyright © 2021 by Sam Crabtree

Published by Crossway
　　　　1300 Crescent Street
　　　　Wheaton, Illinois 60187

Published in association with the literary agency of Wolgemuth & Associates, Inc.

Cover Design: Spencer Fuller, Faceout Studios

First printing 2021

Printed in the United States of America

Unless otherwise indicated, Scripture quotations are from the ESV® Bible (The Holy Bible, English Standard Version®), copyright © 2001 by Crossway, a publishing ministry of Good News Publishers. Used by permission. All rights reserved.

Scripture quotations marked KJV are from the *King James Version* of the Bible. Public domain.

Scripture quotations marked (NIV) are taken from the Holy Bible, New International Version®, NIV®. Copyright © 1973, 1978, 1984, 2011 by Biblica, Inc.™ Used by permission of Zondervan. All rights reserved worldwide. www.zondervan.com. The "NIV" and "New International Version" are trademarks registered in the United States Patent and Trademark Office by Biblica, Inc.™

All emphases in Scripture quotations have been added by the author.

Trade paperback ISBN: 978-1-4335-6931-9
ePub ISBN: 978-1-4335-6933-3
PDF ISBN: 978-1-4335-6932-6
Mobipocket ISBN: 978-1-4335-6933-3

Library of Congress Cataloging-in-Publication Data

Names: Crabtree, Sam, 1950– author.
Title: Practicing thankfulness : cultivating a grateful heart in all circumstances / Sam Crabtree.
Description: Wheaton, Illinois : Crossway, 2021. | Includes bibliographical references and index.
Identifiers: LCCN 2020024965 (print) | LCCN 2020024966 (ebook) | ISBN 9781433569319 (trade paperback) | ISBN 9781433569326 (pdf) | ISBN 9781433569333 (mobipocket) | ISBN 9781433569333 (epub)
Subjects: LCSH: Gratitude—Religious aspects—Christianity.
Classification: LCC BV4647.G8 C73 2021 (print) | LCC BV4647.G8 (ebook) | DDC 241/.4—dc23
LC record available at https://lccn.loc.gov/2020024965
LC ebook record available at https://lccn.loc.gov/2020024966

Crossway is a publishing ministry of Good News Publishers.

VP		31	30	29	28	27	26	25	24	23	22	21
15	14	13	12	11	10	9	8	7	6	5	4	3	2	1

"The righteous flourish like the palm tree
and grow like a cedar in Lebanon. . . .
They still bear fruit in old age;
they are ever full of sap and green."

Psalm 92:12, 14

CONTENTS

Introduction: Where Life Pivots   *11*

1 The Rightness of Gratitude   *15*

2 The Wisdom of Gratitude   *27*

3 Portrait of a Grateful Heart   *35*

4 The Fruitfulness of Gratitude   *43*

5 Dangers of Ingratitude   *51*

6 Thankfulness in Action   *63*

7 Thankfulness and Contentment   *71*

8 Thankfulness and Wonder   *79*

9 Thankfulness and Suffering   *89*

10 Hindrances to Thankfulness   *103*

11 Various Questions about Thankfulness   *109*

12 One Hundred Ways to Be Thankful   *115*

Acknowledged with Thanks   *131*

General Index   *133*

Scripture Index   *137*

WHERE LIFE PIVOTS

Thankfulness is neither trivial nor inconsequential. On this one quality pivots the difference between maturity and immaturity.

What do I mean by pivot? A gate pivots on a hinge so that it swings one way to open the path and another way to shut you out. Wars can pivot on a single battle, so that one side decisively takes the upper hand when the outcome previously was in doubt. Ask Napoleon about Wellington at Waterloo, or Hitler about parachutes at Normandy. The war seemed to be going in one direction, then wham!—things took a sudden and decisive turn.

Gratitude is pivotal in whether I'll be given over to folly. It is decisive.

I dread becoming a bitter old sourpuss in old age. How will I escape it?

More than a mere word, *gratitude* reveals each person's core—his priorities, his presuppositions, his understanding of God and his ways. As Al Mohler puts it, how grateful we are is "the key to understanding what we really believe about God, what we really believe about ourselves, and what we really believe about the world we experience."[1] Accordingly, between gratefulness to God and indifference toward him lies the distinction between wisdom and folly. The pivot. Everyone's entire future swings like a hinge on whether thankfulness is lubricated to swing easily—or if it is ignored, becoming encrusted by the rust and corrosion of our heart's indifference, bitterness, or some self-inflated sense of entitlement.

Thankfulness is not just a religious duty, or a task on a list, or something nice people do, or a simple protocol of good manners to be taught to children. Rather, thankfulness is a powerful force. It wins or loses the war for your future. When practiced, it works toward beauty and produces fruit. When ignored, it works toward ugliness and chokes out life. At stake is the vitality of every human relationship, without exception.

Whether we are aware of it or not, we're always moving toward either the satisfaction of an ultimately unspeakable joy or the pain of excruciating regret. These are the ultimate consequences of either gratitude or ingratitude. This movement toward one or the other may be swift and unmistakably evident, or it may be slow and incremental, nearly invisible—but it always means (wittingly or unwittingly) heaping up either pleasures or sorrows every step of the way.

These dynamics linked directly to gratitude are not optional. They're always in play. A person might choose not to give thanks, but he cannot choose the consequences that will inevitably flow from such a choice.

---

1   Albert Mohler, "Thanksgiving as Theological Act: What Does It Mean to Give Thanks?," AlbertMohler.com, November 23, 2016, https://albertmohler.com/2016/11/23 /thanksgiving-theological-act-mean-give-thanks/.

The workings of thankfulness we're unpacking in these pages have massively broad implications and profoundly deep roots. I repeat: gratitude is downright life-pivoting.

But (you may be thinking) isn't thankfulness already well understood? Isn't it routinely practiced by practically every civil human person around the world? And especially by Christians?

To a certain extent, yes. But just as a fire eventually flickers and dies out if left untended, gratitude can easily weaken and fade away if ignored in a world of distractions, busyness, and painful troubles. Daily life throws cold water on the smoldering embers of gratefulness in our hearts. This book seeks to rekindle that fire.

This book is for two kinds of people. It's for those who have doubts about God's goodness, and who therefore don't often feel grateful. And it's for those who believe God is good but want to grow in their faithful expression of appreciation for that goodness; they want to be more earnest and creative in thanking God as well as thanking those who are instruments in his hands. They're dead serious about wanting to produce the fruit that gratefulness can produce. They're hopeful. The aim here is to minimize your future regret and enlarge your future well-being by fostering your appreciation for all that God is doing.

I assume you already know that you *should* give thanks, and also that you know the basics of how to do it. While we'll explore in this book the influences at work in hearts that are grateful, our main purpose here is finding encouragement and guidance to get on with giving thanks. I want to encourage you to do what you already know is good: *practice thankfulness.*

1

THE RIGHTNESS OF GRATITUDE

Picture yourself in this situation: You've served a long time on death row in a dark and dank medieval dungeon, and your execution is imminent. You smell. No, you stink. It's too dark to see. What must you look like? Your clothing long ago turned to filthy rags, and the slimy stone cell reeks of excrement. A day arrives (remember daylight?) when you hear the footsteps of a guard approaching. A key rattles in the lock, the door swings open, and the guard growls, "Somebody has paid your ransom. You're free."

What?

As you stumble up the steps out of the dungeon, you turn to ask him, "Ransom? What was the ransom price he paid?"

The guard mutters, "Your ransomer had to die in your place."

"When will that happen?" you ask.

"It's done." He waves his hand to keep you climbing the stone stairs.

Stunned, you move toward the last doorway to the outside, where you ask one more question: "How did he die?"

"He died the way he knew he would," the guard replies. "He was butchered alive."

What a price to willingly pay! Wouldn't a proper response be thankfulness multiplied exponentially by amazement? And in your freedom and amazement, wouldn't you run to your friends— to everyone—and enthusiastically exclaim how grateful you are?

Christ pays the price, and is the price, as he himself told us: "The Son of Man came not to be served but to serve, and to give his life as a ransom for many" (Matt. 20:28). He paid the debt he didn't owe for captives who owed a debt they couldn't pay. How fitting for thankfulness to erupt from prisoners thus freed!

Paul described his own salvation—his own "prison escape"— in the following words, where his worship of God begins specifically with thanksgiving:

> *I thank him* who has given me strength, Christ Jesus our Lord, because he judged me faithful, appointing me to his service, though formerly I was a blasphemer, persecutor, and insolent opponent. But I received mercy because I had acted ignorantly in unbelief, and the grace of our Lord overflowed for me with the faith and love that are in Christ Jesus. The saying is trustworthy and deserving of full acceptance, that Christ Jesus came into the world to save sinners, of whom I am the foremost. (1 Tim. 1:12–15)

WE ARE ALWAYS RECIPIENTS

Not only our salvation (which is of incalculable worth, and "deserving of full acceptance"), but *all* that *everyone* has is from the hand of God: "He himself gives to all mankind life and breath and *everything*" (Acts 17:25). God brings us into existence and sustains us (with or without our awareness)—we are thus recipients twenty-four seven. In every aspect of our lives, we're beneficiaries. How fitting, then, for beneficiaries to express flabbergasted appreciation to their benefactor. And how wrongheaded to fail to do so! Such appreciation or lack thereof is not benign, like whether you part your hair on the right or left. No. Like a continental divide determining whether adjacent raindrops flow to the Atlantic or the Pacific, gratitude and ingratitude are a dividing line, bringing vastly different outcomes, as we shall see later in this book.

Paul rhetorically asks the Corinthians (and us), "What do you have that you did not receive?" (1 Cor. 4:7), the correct answer being obvious. If everything we have is received, then the giving of thanks for everything is fitting.

God has not only supplied everything we currently have, but in the future he'll supply everything we will *ever* have. "He who did not spare his own Son but gave him up for us all, how will he not also with him graciously give us all things?" (Rom. 8:32). There will never be an end run around his provision. If God doesn't supply something, we won't have it. There will never be an occasion when we rightly think, "I don't need to thank God for *that*, because it didn't come from him." The soul that is vibrant and aware will gratefully recognize God's gifts more and more, as more and more of his grace arrives.

God owes us none of this. He never has. Not a thing. All that we have is by grace—undeserved, unearned, and even unsolicited. God has supplied each of us with a zillion things we never requested or had the good sense to order in advance. Did you request two kidneys?

Two? Tear ducts that lubricate your eyeballs? An ozone layer around the planet? Synapses in your brain? No. He just gave them to us.

Such incalculable generosity calls for a response. How are we responding? The right response is gratitude—thankfulness. What is gratitude?

> *Gratitude is the divinely given spiritual ability to see grace, and the corresponding desire to affirm it and its giver as good.*

In fact, the New Testament words we translate as "grace" and "gratitude" have the same Greek root.

GOD WASTES NOTHING

God is always at work for his own glory as well as for our good—everywhere, all the time. And he wastes nothing he does; he's working everything for our blessing and benefit: "And we know that for those who love God all things work together for good" (Rom. 8:28). Paul says we *know* this. Do we? Do we act like we know he's working all things without exception for the good of those who love him? I'm sobered by the possibility that my grousing about this or that betrays the reality that maybe I don't love him as much as I claim to. I'm acting like I don't know what Paul says I know—namely, that God is working everything for my good.

The reason God works all things for the good of those who love him is that he himself is good. Therefore, underlying our true gratitude for God's gifts is our amazement at God himself. As John Piper says, "If gratitude is not rooted in the beauty of God before the gift, it is probably disguised idolatry."[1]

---

1   John Piper, *A Godward Life* (Sisters, Oregon: Multnomah, 1997), 213–14.

God is great. God is good. For his greatness we praise him. For his goodness we thank him. His greatness stands alone—he is great whether or not he displays that greatness through any actions we see him take. For his expansive power and wisdom we humbly praise him.

If God were great—awesome in power, mighty in deed—but not kind to us, he would be a monster. He could grind us into a powder and blow us away, and he would be totally just in doing so. He would still be worthy of praise for his terrible powers, but we wouldn't be thankful. But we are thankful, because he applies his unstoppable ability toward accomplishing our everlasting joy in him, confident that even through our affliction he's "preparing for us an eternal weight of glory beyond all comparison" (2 Cor. 4:17). God is good, not just great. Believers fear him *and* like him! We praise him *and* thank him.

In fact, this is what marks the distinction between believers and demons. Demons know theology. They can recite Scripture. They know the claims of Christ, and they know his identity. Sooner or later they will bend the knee. *But they don't like him.* Demons can praise him, and they fear him; they recognize his awesome power. But they take no pleasure in him, and they never thank him.

In contrast, believers enjoy God and they thank him. "The real difference between a Christian and a non-Christian," Tremper Longman writes, "is that the former gives thanks to God."[2] I recently interviewed a Chinese woman through an interpreter.

2   Tremper Longman, *How to Read the Psalms* (Downers Grove, IL: InterVarsity Press, 1988), 144.

When she fled China and examined Western culture, trying to understand differences between Buddhism and Christianity, she made this generalization about Westerners: "They don't practice thanksgiving, so they must not be Christians." I use her generalization as a mirror; I look in there and wonder if I see myself.

MORE EVERY MOMENT

Because God is always and everywhere at work doing good, there's never a time when God-honoring hearts are licensed to lapse from the soul-enriching practice of thankfulness. Every moment is another opportunity to observe, embrace, and appreciate with gratefulness the wondrous workings of God, who works wonders even in ordinary things—as in, for example, "the way of an eagle in the sky, / the way of a serpent on a rock, / the way of a ship on the high seas, / and the way of a man with a virgin" things which "are too wonderful" for us to fully comprehend (Prov. 30:18–19).

Since God is working all things together for the good of those who love him, it's entirely fitting that we be "giving thanks always and for everything to God the Father in the name of our Lord Jesus Christ" (Eph. 5:20). *Always and for everything*—what a sweeping assertion! When it comes to the extent of our gratitude, many people cite only 1 Thessalonians 5:18, "give thanks in all circumstances," pointing out that it says *in* everything, not *for* everything.

But 1 Thessalonians 5:18 isn't the only verse in the Bible about giving thanks. The Bible has much more to say. Ephesians 5:20 *does* say "for everything." Thankful for what? Everything. And when? Always.

THE RIGHTNESS OF GRATITUDE

So the thankfulness of Ephesians 5:20 expands that of 1 Thessalonians 5:18 into something far bigger—not just *in* everything, but *for* everything.

Ponder "*in* everything give thanks." A Hungarian proverb says, "When the bridge is gone, the narrowest plank becomes precious." I suppose that's one way to embrace a 1 Thessalonians 5:18 approach to life; in the collapse of the bridge, we express gratefulness for the part of the bridge that remains. But are we also thankful for the part that collapsed?

Likewise, in cold Minnesota winters folks jest about how the mosquitoes aren't bad. Okay, but can the same folks also thank God for the mosquitoes when they're thick?

From Ephesians 5, we're instructed to give thanks when the mosquitoes are thick and also for the part of the bridge that collapsed. God is at work in both the presence and the absence of mosquitoes, and he's at work not only in the bridge portion that survives but also in the collapse of the rest. He's working *all* things for our good.

This is a difficult doctrine, cutting across our natural impulses. It requires faith in the completely sovereign God who isn't done working all things, including mosquitoes and collapsed bridges, for the good of those who love him.

I don't speak of collapsed bridges lightly. From my kitchen window I can see a ten-lane interstate highway bridge that crosses the Mississippi River. It replaces a bridge in that same location that collapsed in 2007, killing thirteen and injuring 145 others, many seriously. Are we to give thanks for *that*?

We need to understand that God is always working. Even the things that grieve God, the events that threaten to crush us, the things that elicit his compassion and comfort for his people—those things are not accidents or flaws in the plan. They come from the same God who loved us enough to send his Son to die, the same God who says he will never leave us or forsake us. In the deepest pain, we can still give thanks because our God is still here with us and he is working all things for our good, even it if is difficult for us to see how on this side of eternity.

This kind of radical thankfulness simply isn't possible unless we are convinced that God is always working and that he is always good. Everything that afflicts or wounds and traumatizes us—including a collapsed bridge, your cancer, your miscarriage, your spouse's adultery, the death of your child, the loss of your job, or the collapse of the economy—is under the total control of a God who is unchangeably *for* all who are in Christ.

Paul Eickstadt, a fifty-one-year-old trucker, was on that bridge when it collapsed and killed him. Was that the end of his life? Yes, but only in a narrow sense. In another sense, that death was not the end of his life. On the banks above the river where his truck fell amid the rubble is a memorial with these words:

I was a traveler
Across the country far and wide.
I heard the mountain's testimony
And saw the skies declare His glory.

Along the highways I traveled
Till concrete and steel collapsed.
Though crushed and buried
I am still alive!

As man's work failed me
My Savior stood by me.
Consider the work of Jesus Christ
For his love endures forever

To conclude that when Paul Eickstadt died God had failed him is to conclude that God was finished with Paul. No way. God was not and is not finished. Ingratitude prejudges God before more of the story is revealed. God is not done. He never is.

AS NATURAL AS BREATHING

If we're to be thankful "always and for everything," then we're to be thankful for every breath, since God himself "gives to all mankind life and breath and everything" (as we saw in Acts 17:25). Oh, that gratitude would come as naturally to me as breathing!

It's not that we need more for which to be thankful. Rather, we should naturally be more thankful for what we already have. God serves us with every breath we take—which is about twenty thousand times per day. And that's just breathing. He also serves us with every blink of the eye, every beat of the heart, every multiplication of every cell, every brain wave, and every subatomic particle zooming around in our bodies countless times each millisecond.

And that's just our bodies. He's also holding our massive sun in its position at the just-right distance from the earth to give us weather that's livable for us and suitable for producing our food. Meanwhile he's stirring and cleaning the oceans and the atmosphere with lunar tides and wind currents. He's sweeping dangerous asteroids out of their supersonic earthbound trajectories by having them absorbed by our atmosphere or by the moon's nearby gravity field.

He gives the capacity to reason, to recall, to relate, and—thank God—to repent. He gives us our frame, our forefathers, our fingerprints, our sex chromosomes, and the wombs in which he knits us. And he so loves us that he gives us his Son, that whoever believes in him would not perish but have everlasting life (John 3:16). He gives us promises, hope, adversity (more on that later), and faith.

There are plenty of blessings to go around—more than we could ever imagine. The human population, no matter how large, will never run out of material for which to give thanks.

There's no stealing of gratitude; it's impossible. Just because one person has given thanks for something doesn't mean another person can't give thanks for the same thing—over and over. One person's gratitude can never diminish the gratitude of others. In fact, it works the other way around. Gratitude tends to spread, multiply, and intensify like a contagion. Covet gratitude, earnestly desire to get good at it. Then spread it.

———

It is fitting—morally appropriate, as well as emotionally joyful—to thank God: "It is good to give thanks to the LORD" (Ps. 92:1). Thankfulness to God is *good*. It suits God, and it outfits the worshiper for relating rightly to God and to all of life.

Thankfulness doesn't earn us any favor with God, but is evidence that his favor is already being enjoyed. Accordingly, giving thanks is not a religious "work" that piles up merit in our account. Gratitude springs from faith, and faith is a gift (Eph. 2:8–9).

Therefore, if we're grateful, we should be grateful for being grateful. A heart of gratitude was given to us as a gift. Thank the giver.

Practicing thankfulness is not just a matter of mustering up the good manners at Christmas to thank Grandma for that new sweater you'll never wear in public. Thankfulness is all about the absolute and total lordship of God, his sovereignty over all things, and his kindness in using his almighty power to work all things for our good—while our enlivened hearts gratefully recognize him as the source of it all.

I've attended thousands of prayer meetings over the years, and our prayers can tend to gravitate toward petitions. Petitions are not wrong; God invites them. But the giving of thanks can easily get edged to the margins. Thanksgiving deserves a proportionately weighty place in our prayer lives. Giving glad-hearted thanks fuels confidence that God is caring for us right now, and it enlarges our hope that he will keep on carrying us to completion. "Hope grows in the soil of gratitude."[3]

3 David Little, *Imago Hearts* newsletter, August 7, 2019.

2

THE WISDOM OF GRATITUDE

Because gratitude is so perfectly right—so completely appropriate in the God-supplied, God-blessed reality in which we find ourselves—thankfulness is the loftiest form of mental activity our minds can engage in. I agree with G. K. Chesterton, who said, "I would maintain that thanks are the highest form of thought, and that gratitude is happiness doubled by wonder."[1]

Wise people make it a priority to keep thankfulness in mind. Or to say it another way, gratefulness is the mindset of the wise.

Genuine gratitude is rooted in definite consciousness of God's presence and provision, including salvation, just as David experienced and prayed: "I will render thank offerings to you. / For you have delivered my soul from death, / yes, my feet from falling, / that I may walk before God / in the light of life" (Ps. 56:12–13).

THINKING AND THANKING

Generally, feelings stem from thinking. Feeling grateful erupts from thinking rightly about God's good provision. Every good

---

1   G. K. Chesterton, "Christmas and Salesmanship," in *The Collected Works of G. K. Chesterton* (San Francisco: Ignatius Press, 2012), 37:205.

and perfect gift comes from God. Our problem is that in our human frailty and inability to see all things, we can sometimes be inclined to think that some of the circumstances coming to us from God are not good but bad—certainly not perfect. In fact, we sometimes consider all of them bad and none of them good. We err in thinking that way. And when our thoughts err in that way, our feelings follow. We don't feel grateful.

But people who think, thank. Or more precisely, people who think rightly thank humbly. "Thank you" conveys not only humility, but understanding. True understanding and humility always go together.

This same mix of understanding and humility is displayed in Jesus the Son of God. We learn of Jesus that "all things were made through him, and without him was not any thing made that was made" (John 1:3); and again, that "by him all things were created, in heaven and on earth," and that "he is before all things, and in him all things hold together" (Col. 1:16–17). The Son was intimately involved in the creation of all things, yet he thanks the Father (as in Matt. 11:25; Luke 10:21; John 11:41), for he understands his role of submission to the Father. Within the Trinity, God thanks God—humbly and in complete understanding. (This is part of the mystery of the Trinity.)

Again, those who think, thank. Or as Cindy Lubar Bishop cleverly restates the famous line, "I am, therefore I thank."[2] Or consider this further adaptation: He is, therefore I thank.

---

2 Cindy Lubar Bishop in *Everyday Gratitude*, ed. Saorise McClory, Kristi Nelson, and Margaret Wakeley (North Adams, MA: Storey Publishing, 2018), 201.

A mind that's truly clear-thinking will always recognize the rightness of gratitude. After all, thanksgiving gives credit where credit is due. How sensible. The universe is right side up when the one who does the work is the one who gets the credit. It is God who gives life, breath, and everything else, so he always deserves credit.

A person who consistently thanks God is therefore being supremely rational. And who in his right mind doesn't want to be rational? As we will see later when we look at Romans 1, those who refuse to thank God are guilty of suppressing the truth by their unrighteousness, and they end up confused, foolish, darkened, and given over to a wide array of wickedness and perversion.

So be sane. Give thanks.

The thankful mind is able to hold on to true hope. Whereas thankfulness looks *back* in faith that nothing in our life has been wasted (God never wastes a thing), hope looks *forward* in faith that nothing *will* be wasted. Therefore, thanksgiving brightens one's hopefulness. Every backward glance that marvels at the milestones of God's past provision helps us look forward with more hope for divine provision yet to come.

Such hope need never run out. If gratitude were money, you could endlessly print your own bills. There's no law against it. The thankful person taps into a spring that never runs dry, and never can—because God is inexhaustibly generous.

The truly thankful mind also gives no credence to luck. When things go well for you, it simply won't do to say you were lucky. For one thing, to credit mere luck robs God of the thanks and honor he deserves. For another, there's no such thing as luck. The person who claims luck is on his side reveals that he's not as rational as he might think. As R. C. Sproul states,

In a universe governed by God there are no chance events. Indeed, there is no such thing as chance. Chance does not exist. It is merely a word we use to describe mathematical possibilities. But chance itself has no power because it has no being. Chance is not an entity that can influence reality. Chance is not a thing. It is nothing.[3]

Gratitude need not and must not hinge solely upon the presence or absence of certain circumstances (triumph versus trouble), but on the presence of God. Our God isn't finished producing fruit through your circumstances, no matter how painful they may be. If Lazarus has died, God is not done. If your bridge has collapsed, he is not done. If the mosquitoes have swarmed, he is not done.

Paul reminds us that "he who began a good work in you will bring it to completion at the day of Jesus Christ" (Phil. 1:6). What is God doing *now* in your life to carry on to completion that which he has begun? In this very moment he is using your current set of circumstances as one link in the unbreakable chain of links forged by his unrelenting love and infinite wisdom to accomplish for you the unspeakably valuable privilege of being conformed to the image of his Son. Therefore we're wise to be thankful not only for the promise that he'll complete what he has begun—and not only for the chain of completion as a whole—but also for every individual link in that chain.

The clear and grateful mind also recognizes the danger of thinking gratitude is something we *owe* God. While in one

---

3 R. C. Sproul, *Essential Truths of the Christian Faith* (Wheaton, IL: Tyndale House, 1992), 66.

sense we do "owe" God for everything we have, it's foolish to think we can repay him for what he has given us. With what would we pay him? With something he has already given us in the first place? Such thinking would lead to an endless cycle of growing indebtedness. His grace *pays* debts; it does not increase them. We thank him not because we're obligated, but because it's our pleasure to give him honor by giving thanks.

GRATITUDE IN THE RIGHT DIRECTION

Compare the action verb *thanking* with some other action verb—*pushing*, for example. Thanking and pushing are similar in that they both act upon something. Both thanking and pushing assume and require an object, a recipient of the thanking or the pushing. You don't just push, you push *something*. And you don't just thank, you thank *someone*.

It would be irrational to say that practicing gratefulness is just a feeling, without conveying any of that feeling to a benefactor—just as it would be irrational to say that pushing is a "feeling" when you aren't actually pushing on something. "I feel pushy" means nothing unless you push something. Similarly, you can't merely "honor"; you have to honor something or someone. The very honor must have an object. So it is with thanking. You can't merely feel thankful, but must express that gratitude *to* someone.

"The worst moment for an atheist," G. K. Chesterton wrote, "is when he is really thankful and has no one to thank."[4] I think what he means by "really thankful" is a conscious awareness that

---

4   G. K. Chesterton, paraphrasing poet Dante Gabriel Rossetti, *St. Francis of Assisi*, in *The Collected Works of G. K. Chesterton* (San Francisco: Ignatius, 1986), 2:75.

a person is not—and cannot be—self-made. Therefore he owes his existence, his preservation, his sustenance, his circumstances, and his happiness to someone other than himself. But to whom? The atheist suppresses the possibility that his very life is owed entirely to the God who revealed himself in nature and in the Bible and claims to supply the atheist with life, and breath, and everything else (Acts 17:25).

During the American Thanksgiving holiday, the secular media is typically filled with thankful sentiments. That is, they're filled with the echoes of thanksgiving, without confessing the genuine thing. They *feel* something, and they want to call that feeling thankfulness, but they can't bring themselves to admit that it's God to whom they should express their thanks. I've heard well-intentioned adults ask children, "What are you thankful for?" Failing to ask "To whom are you thankful?" places the emphasis on the what, not the who.

To what shall we compare an atheist at Thanksgiving? Imagine an Olympic gymnast on the balance beam who beautifully completes all her moves. After the performance, as she's being interviewed, she tries to give the impression that no beam was ever actually there—that all her moves were performed in midair. She even refers to the event as simply "the balance," trying hard to ignore what everyone intuits and plainly sees: the event is called the balance *beam*, and she could do no balancing whatsoever unless there was something to balance *on*.

Secularists want to get in on the warm fuzzies of thanksgiving without acknowledging that there's a God holding everything up, providing all the things we feel so warm and fuzzy about. The secularist wants to be thankful without giving thanks to the actual provider. Just as the gymnast desires to win a prize for being such a wonderful balancer, the secularist wants credit for being so thankful, all the while suppressing the grounds for his gratefulness—denying that there's any such thing as providence.

Take a moment to reflect on how the Heidelberg Catechism of 1563 defines God's providence:

> Providence is the almighty and ever present power of God by which he upholds, as with his hand, heaven and earth and all creatures, and so rules them that leaf and blade, rain and drought, fruitful and lean years, food and drink, health and sickness, prosperity and poverty—all things, in fact—come to us not by chance but from his fatherly hand.[5]

Others who wouldn't claim to be atheists will admit that thanksgiving should go to *something* or to *someone*, but they fall short of fully recognizing the "fatherly hand" of the true divine benefactor.

I heard a man who would number himself among the educational elite state on the radio that at Thanksgiving time his family reads great poems and Buddhist prayers. Animists and cultists have their corresponding vain idols, manmade and powerless, as they intone, "Let us thank the favorable winds that have blown across this nation." Astrologers who thank their lucky stars ought to look beyond the stars to the one who made them. The sun worshipers of Egypt should look beyond the sun to the Son who sustains it. Poets who wax eloquent about geese formations and

---

5 Heidelberg Catechism, Question 27, as updated by the Christian Reformed Church (Grand Rapids, MI: CRC Publications, 1988).

cornucopia of colorful vegetables should look beyond them to the living Word, the true vine, the bread of life.

As these hollow professors of thanksgiving are given media time every November, year after year, I'd love to hear an interviewer dare to ask such a person a simple follow-up question: "If the one who does the work gets the glory, who should get the credit for the wonderful benefits you just mentioned?" And then do some further probing: "Isn't it irrational to 'give thanks' to no one in particular? If there's no one to *get* thanks, isn't it ridiculous to give it?"

If we enjoy the world, and chalk it up to a combination of random forces over time, we can consider our conclusions of purposelessness to be empty ramblings. But man cannot live with purposelessness, any more than a gymnast can levitate. Something in all of us knows that we cannot take credit for all the benefits around us. And yet humanity's fallen nature and truth suppression (see Rom. 1:18) blinds so many to the common grace of almighty God as the source of all blessings. So we give thanks to thin air, or karma, or our lucky stars, or the Force.

May it never be so. With clear minds, we have the privilege instead to wholeheartedly give thanks to the immortal, invisible God, and to remember and retell what he has so awesomely accomplished: "We give thanks to you, O God; / we give thanks, for your name is near. / We recount your wondrous deeds" (Ps. 75:1).

In the next few pages, we'll paint a portrait of a grateful heart.

3

PORTRAIT OF A
GRATEFUL HEART

Saying "thank you"—whether to God or to other people—may at first seem like a social formality, a rule in an etiquette manual, a polite chore, or a mannerly discipline that can be void of much delight. It can be a hurried and insincere obligation at the tail end of a social transaction. "Thanks for the fruitcake." But genuine gratitude overflows from a heart that's tuned in to true reality.

If we're without gratitude, the way we're responding to our circumstances is already lacking delight. This is evident even in the occasional fly-by remarks of gratitude we may dutifully offer others; we're just gutting it out stoically, sending out thank-you notes after the wedding because it's a (sigh) duty that civilized people somehow manage to check off their list of obligations. We want to stay in society's good graces by doing our duty in order to justify our claim to goodness. If it stems from obligation, not grace, it is joyless.

More than a task to check off a list, thankfulness is the outlook of a certain kind of heart.

What kind?

TRANSFORMED BY CHRIST

Heartfelt thankfulness stems from Christ. He wills it, and he makes it possible. As we've seen in 1 Thessalonians 5:18, we're to give thanks in all circumstances because "this is the will of God *in Christ Jesus*" for us. God wills our thankfulness, and he wills it "in Christ." He accomplishes our thankful hearts through the transformative work accomplished in our hearts by his word when it dwells in us:

> Let the word of Christ dwell in you richly, teaching and admonishing one another in all wisdom, singing psalms and hymns and spiritual songs, *with thankfulness* in your hearts to God. And whatever you do, in word or deed, do everything in the name of the Lord Jesus, *giving thanks* to God the Father through him. (Col. 3:16–17)

When you read that verse, pay attention to "whatever you do" and "everything." In the doing of *whatever* we do, we're to be full of gratitude. Our hearts pivot on the word of Christ. Either they swivel toward him in wonder and gratitude and affection, or they swivel away from him in stubborn, truth-suppressing pride or apathetic indifference. It's through Christ and in the name of Christ that the grateful heart erupts with thankfulness to the Father for all things, especially the word of Christ that indwells the heart richly.

Thankful hearts don't use small measuring cups. Word-enriched, faith-filled, Christ-following hearts will abound in gratitude: "Therefore, as you received Christ Jesus the Lord, so walk in him, rooted and built up in him and established in the faith, just as you were taught, *abounding in thanksgiving*" (Col. 2:6–7).

The degree to which I'm not thankful is the degree to which I should ask myself if I'm as rooted and built up in Christ as I may think I am.

It's essential that we see the fundamental primacy of being rooted and built up in Christ as the spring or fountainhead of thanksgiving. We're to be "rooted and built up in him and established in the faith, just as you were taught, abounding in thanksgiving" (Col. 2:7).

We encounter a serious problem: "Give thanks" is a biblical command, but it's a command that the flesh *cannot* obey. "For the mind that is set on the flesh is hostile to God, for it does not submit to God's law; indeed, it cannot" (Rom. 8:7). So Christ died to create a thankful heart in us, to generate in us what otherwise isn't there.

Gratitude toward God is thus an indication that a person is spiritually alive, awake, alert. Habitual thankfulness toward God surely indicates a heart that loves and trusts God. "A spirit of thankfulness," said Billy Graham, "is one of the most distinctive marks of a Christian whose heart is attuned to the Lord. Thank God in the midst of trials and every persecution."[1]

By contrast, thanklessness raises the question of where one's affection lies. A person will not be fully and truly thankful unless God first does a work in the heart. Rooted in God, thankfulness itself is from God, through him, and to him, since "from him and through him and to him are *all things*" (Rom. 11:36)—including thankful hearts.

---

1 Billy Graham, "In His Own Words: Billy Graham on Thankfulness," The Billy Graham Library website, November 21, 2012, https://billygrahamlibrary.org/in-his-own-words -billy-graham-on-thankfulness/.

If you're thankful to God, be thankful for your thankfulness, because he's the one making it possible in your heart.

GROWING IN GRATITUDE

In a sense, a heart of thankfulness is a rudimentary first step in Christian living, but it's a step that never disappears from the believer's repertoire.

It's like breathing. Breathing is one of the first things we earnestly desire for a newborn to do, but we never want it to stop. We don't say, "Okay, now that you've breathed, let's move on to other things and leave breathing behind." Or think of how we commend babies for taking their first steps, yet we don't expect them at that point to stop walking and move on instead to other signs of development; we expect them to keep on walking the rest of their lives. Similarly, gratitude is a basic early step in the progress of the disciple, and never to be abandoned as a way of life.

A heart of thankfulness is an entry point. We're to enter God's gates with thanksgiving: "Enter his gates with thanksgiving, / and his courts with praise! / Give thanks to him; bless his name!" (Ps. 100:4). If we enter his gates with thanksgiving, perhaps we can think of thanksgiving as the key to the gate. After entering, we don't stop, but keep on keeping on in giving thanks—not out of raw duty, but out of amazed hearts, always keeping the key in the ready.

By entering his gates we have access to God. We take the first step with thanks, and then give thanks with every subsequent step along the route to the Father. No wonder, then, that Daniel practiced thankfulness before interpreting the king's dream (Dan. 2:23). No wonder the twenty-four elders give thanks when God's temple in heaven is opened (Rev. 11:16–19).

No wonder that Jesus, before he broke bread, gave thanks (Luke 22:17–19; Matt. 26:27), and that he gave thanks before teaching his disciples privately (Luke 10:21). Before freeing Lazarus from the grave, Jesus began by giving thanks (John 11:41–42). He didn't pause to give thanks, as though this was an interruption of more important matters; rather, giving thanks was a necessary first action, part and parcel of the beauty he was performing.

HUMBLE AND DEPENDENT

Thankfulness depends upon an awareness of dependence. Awareness of dependence is akin to humility. God resists the proud, but gives grace to the humble. If there's one thing we don't need, it's God's resistance, and if there's one thing we do need, it's enabling grace.

The humbly grateful soul is grateful to God for making him grateful to God. God does the transforming work, turning our hearts from ungrateful to grateful, and we then give him thanks for being the worker in that process. We're dependent upon him, and aware of our dependence.

Humility means embracing the role of external provision. We recognize that we're completely dependent on God and others, and we look for ways to acknowledge them with appreciation.

Have you ever noticed how so much of what we enjoy is accomplished for us through the pain of someone else? We're all dependent upon others for so many things.

- Your mother and those serving her went through a great deal while you were pretty passive during your birth.

- National freedoms cost many soldiers their lives or disabilities.
- Early in American history, patriots pledged their lives, fortunes, and sacred honor to give birth to a nation of principle.
- Many workers died in the construction of the Panama Canal to provide products we now take for granted.
- Driving instructors give of their adrenaline so novices can be licensed to drive.
- Police officers routinely put themselves in harm's way in order to keep order for everyone else.
- Firefighters risk their lives to protect our attics full of junk.
- Down through the centuries, faithful messengers of the gospel have risked all they possessed so that you and I might have the opportunity to respond to the claims and identity of Jesus.

As we have opportunity, we produce fruit by directly thanking those whom we depend on. And we can thank God for those we owe gratitude to who are long dead. We can speak well of their sacrifice to others still living.

Thankful people recognize their own dependence, and speak up with gratefulness. And just as our thankfulness depends upon an awareness of dependence, so it also fosters even greater awareness of dependence, in an endlessly joyful cycle.

Even strong people are dependent upon others. In the 1950s, Paul Anderson was crowned the World's Strongest Man having lifted 6,270 pounds! I was in the auditorium when he lifted—and carried around for several steps—a reinforced table with eight college varsity football players sitting on it. He also performed other feats of strength, after which he announced to the audience of around five thousand that he couldn't take one single step unless God gave him the strength.

Since even strong people are dependent upon others, it's entirely fitting for all of us to give thanks. Strong or weak, we all owe whatever measure of strength we have to a mighty God.

Next we'll ask, What fruit is produced by gratitude?

4

THE FRUITFULNESS
OF GRATITUDE

Giving thanks is not just polite societal etiquette. Practicing thankfulness is productive! The practice of thankfulness fosters outcomes and brings to pass things that otherwise wouldn't happen. That's the way God designed it to function.

With gratitude, everyone wins. You get more delight in God, God gets more glory from you, and people around you find enjoyment from your words and gestures of appreciation.

The consequences flowing either from thankfulness or from ingratitude are universal and not optional. No one can escape the fundamental order God has wired into the universe, and that includes the dynamics pertaining to gratitude and ingratitude.

The well-being of one's soul is at stake. As Jon Bloom rightly says, "Gratitude is both a vital indicator of our soul's health and a powerful defender of our soul's happiness."[1] In the bouquet of flowers that grow from the soil of the believer's transformed heart,

---

1   Jon Bloom, "Fill Your Wandering Heart with Thankfulness," desiringGod.org, November 18, 2018, https://www.desiringgod.org/articles/fill-your-wandering-heart-with-thankfulness.

gratefulness is surely one that blooms the loveliest. Expressing gratitude is so simple yet so powerful. It has a transforming power that's not to be underestimated.

The giving of thanks bears fruit. It is *productive*. Gratitude creates something that wasn't there before. As the Roman statesman Cicero wrote, "There is nothing which I can esteem more highly than being and appearing grateful. For this one virtue is not only the greatest, but is also the parent of all the other virtues."[2] Other virtues are the children of gratitude.

Abandoning self-righteous efforts to justify ourselves before God and instead giving thanks for the righteous standing that is ours in Christ fosters the development of additional good habits and patterns. For example, thankfulness liberates from envy. It's virtually impossible to be envious and thankful simultaneously. Gratefulness has the same obliterating effect on other temptations, like jealousy, self-pity, and malice.

Gratefulness has a sanctifying effect on things like marriage and mealtime. That's why Paul condemns those "who forbid marriage and require abstinence from foods that God created to be *received with thanksgiving* by those who believe and know the truth," and then reminds Timothy that "everything created by God is good, and nothing is to be rejected *if it is received with thanksgiving*, for it is made holy by the word of God and prayer" (1 Tim. 4:3–5). The holiness of marriage and of our meals is recognized through thanksgiving, and missed without it.

---

2 Marcus Tullius Cicero, *Pro Plancio*, University of Chicago Perseus Project, Perseus Digital Library, section 80, accessed October 24, 2019, http://perseus.uchicago.edu/perseus-cgi /citequery3.pl?dbname=LatinAugust2012&getid=1&query=Cic.%20Planc.%2080#80.

Gratitude gives the Spirit a wider range inside our hearts, as Andrew Murray tells us: "Let us thank God heartily. . . . Thanksgiving will draw our hearts out to God and keep us engaged with Him; it will take our attention from ourselves and give the Spirit room in our hearts."[3]

Thanksgiving provides sentry duty for our inward being. We guard our soul with humble alertness as we obey Colossians 4:2: "Continue steadfastly in prayer, being watchful in it *with thanksgiving*." Practicing thankfulness guards and nourishes the heart in dimensions that can't be nourished any other way. That's why thankfulness is not optional.

THANKFULNESS AND HAPPINESS

One might ask, Does thankfulness *produce* happiness? Or is it the other way around? Does happiness erupt in thankfulness? It's the old chicken-and-egg question. But maybe they're two ingredients in the same casserole, with their individual flavors seeping into each other. Thankfulness and happiness are like two wheels on the same axle; they go together. And when they're working together, you can go places.

In 2003, the American Psychological Association published research that demonstrated that a conscious focus on blessings may have emotional and interpersonal benefits.[4] Three groups were instructed to keep journals—one group recording any or

---

3 Andrew Murray, *Living a Prayerful Life* (Minneapolis: Bethany House, 1983), 63–64.

4 Robert A. Emmons and Michael E. McCullough, "Counting Blessings versus Burdens: An Experimental Investigation of Gratitude and Subjective Well-Being in Daily Life," *Journal of Personality and Social Psychology* 84, no. 2 (2003): 377–89.

all events, the second group recording negative experiences, and the third group compiling a list of things for which they were grateful. The gratitude group felt better about their lives as a whole, and were more optimistic in their expectations for the upcoming week. Practicing conscious gratefulness seemed to show a positive correlation with greater happiness.

That's not to say gratitude guarantees perfect health or trouble-free living this side of glory. Furthermore, godless positivity is shortsighted; it will eventually collapse when it collides with tragic and painful circumstances. But the research cited nevertheless supports the assertion that gratitude is good for overall morale.

As the Swiss-British philosopher Alain de Botton wrote, "Every time we feel satisfied with what we have, we can be counted as rich, however little we may actually possess."[5] Christian psychologist Gary Collins goes so far as to say, "The core ingredient of mental health is gratitude."[6] Growth in gratitude reduces inner stress and produces peace. Who knows? You might be one thankful thought away from experiencing unprecedented satisfaction in the pervasive goodness of God.

The writers of the Bible didn't need studies in psychological journals in order to know that "the cheerful of heart has a continual feast" (Prov. 15:15).

REPENTANCE INSTEAD OF HARDNESS OF HEART

Another benefit of practicing thankfulness is that it leads to repentance. We see this in Paul's progression of thought in the

---

5   Alain De Botton, *Status Anxiety* (New York: Vintage, 2004), 43.
6   Gary Collins, "Gratitude Is Good for You," *Christian Herald*, February 1984, 51.

first two chapters of Romans, where thankfulness is equated with acknowledging God, then equated as well with *not* presuming on God's kindness. Paul asks, "Do you presume on the riches of his kindness and forbearance and patience, not knowing that God's kindness is meant to lead you to repentance?" (Rom. 2:4).

The person who is actively grateful for God's demonstrated kindness will understandably be more ready to repent. We can follow Paul's logic here:

1. Sinners like us need to repent.

2. God's kindness leads to the repentance that sinners like us need.

3. The grateful heart sees that kindness, and gives thanks for it.

4. In contrast, presuming upon the riches of his kindness impedes the needed repentance. Presuming that God will continue being kind to us in the absence of our repentance is a grave mistake.

5. The impenitent become increasingly hardened.

We could paraphrase Paul's teaching to say, "Heart gratitude for the riches of God's kindness, forbearance, and patience opens the pathway to repentance, instead of hardening the heart."

Thankfulness honors God while enlivening and sweetening our communion with him. In contrast, to presume that we deserve God's blessings is to risk hardening. The lesson is clear: practice thankfulness while you have opportunity! Pivot toward sweet gladness in God's kindness, or else your heart will pivot toward sourness and hardness toward him.

THANKING OTHERS

Another positive reward of practicing thankfulness is knowing that your gracious words expressing thanks to others can have a restorative healing effect: "Gracious words are like a honeycomb, / sweetness to the soul and health to the body" (Prov. 16:24). This is true for both the speaker and the hearer of those gracious words. Thankfulness is energy-giving to the thankful as well as to those around them, adorning speech and brightening the environment.

The thank-you cards you see in the ubiquitous greeting card racks found in stores and restaurants will commonly express sentiments like these: "You brightened my day"; "You are so thoughtful"; "You made a difference"; "It was huge." These all point to the significance of some gift or service, and how much that gift or service meant. Why do cards like that sell in the quantities they do? The hefty demand for thank-you cards stems from the pleasure it gives the sender to offer genuine thanks. They enjoy expressing their warmth toward the giver.

Why express thanks? Chiefly, it is to honor God, but secondarily—yet in no way unimportantly— it is because many people *need* your expressions of appreciation for their own morale, hope, and perseverance. To not thank them is to deprive them of the morale boost they might need that very day.

JOY AND THANKSGIVING

Throughout Scripture we see the understandable connection between rejoicing and gratitude, as in the concluding verse in Psalm 97: "Rejoice in the LORD, O you righteous, / *and* give thanks to his holy name!" (v. 12). Consider Paul's elated words to the Thessalonians: "How can we thank God enough for you in return for all the joy we have in the presence of our God because of you?" (1 Thess. 3:9 NIV). Joy leads to gratitude. The simple process looks like this:

gladness and rejoicing → thanksgiving

Glad rejoicing is God's intention for our days. Moses was in the will of God when he prayed, "Satisfy us in the morning with your steadfast love, / that we may rejoice and be glad all our days" (Ps. 90:14). Written as a formula, it could look something like this:

God's steadfast love → our satisfaction → gladness and rejoicing

God, who is love, fastens his love upon us in mighty deeds and sufficient revelation. Our God-awakened powers of observation recognize his love as love, and our hearts find it satisfying. This satisfaction overflows in irrepressible daily hopefulness and purposefulness, amounting to gladness. Then we easily say with Paul, "How can we thank God enough?" and give our best efforts in doing just that.

Does such satisfaction and joy mean that we have no more longings? No. But our longings for the right things—for God's will, God's honor, and God himself—will be increasingly satisfied forever.

Moses wasn't naive about all this. He didn't think a life of daily gladness was a life sanitized of all suffering. We see this in the very next words of his prayer to God: "Make us glad for as many days as you have afflicted us, / and for as many years as we have seen evil" (Ps. 90:15). Moses was clear: It is God who afflicts. But when he afflicts, he is not done. God doesn't leave us in affliction, nor waste the affliction. The affliction is designed to produce fruit and gladness. (We'll explore this more deeply later.)

We know that drinking plenty of water is healthy, and not drinking enough water presents problems. So, too, *not* practicing gratitude introduces deadly hazards.

5

DANGERS OF INGRATITUDE

It's almost impossible to overestimate the tragic outcomes of failing to be grateful. The very dividing line between glory and dishonor is whether a person gives thanks or not. Idolatry itself springs from thanklessness toward our Creator—whose "invisible attributes, namely, his eternal power and divine nature, have been clearly perceived, ever since the creation of the world, in the things that have been made" (Rom. 1:20).

In contrast to the honor, sweetness, joy, and health produced by a right response—genuine thankfulness—to the provider of all things, thanklessness toward the provider has unraveled paradise, ruined peace in the human race, and put the entire planet under a curse of enmity, decay, pain in childbearing, thorns, and death (Gen. 3:15–19). Specifically, as we'll explore in this chapter, thanklessness is at the root of homosexuality, covetousness, envy, murder, and a whole array of foolish and faithless derailments, as clearly stated in Romans 1:21–32.

Moreover, ingratitude toward others ruins relationships. No man is an island, or so goes the well-worn idiom. We're not in a vacuum when we fail to practice thankfulness. Our lives are connected to others. Our behavior patterns exert influence. Thankfulness has rescued relationships, and thanklessness has ruined them. A forgotten thank-you can feel like a forgotten relationship. Relationships flourish where even the most ordinary and mundane benefits are appreciated.

Because even a child can say thank you, we might be tempted to think gratefulness is not a characteristic of maturity. But it is. To fail at practicing thankfulness is to stymie growth and block progress in faith.

Because character qualities tend to cluster together, running in packs, it doesn't work to try to develop one lone character quality while remaining sloppy about others. Bad qualities will drag everything down. A thankless person is weakened and made less fit for serving God's will and purpose. The same goes for a thankless church.

UGLY DESTRUCTIVENESS

Although the outcomes of practicing thankfulness are clearly beautiful and fruitful, our complaining hearts do not gravitate automatically toward gratitude. One way God might be pleased to awaken our callous, indifferent hearts is to alert us to the ugly and destructive consequences of ingratitude.

Again, the dynamics involved are not optional. No one's spirit can remain neutral. There can be no fence sitting. Either we give thanks and reap the beneficial by-products, or we don't give thanks, and thereby accrue painful and regrettable consequences to ourselves. You can intentionally choose to not be grateful, and you can unintentionally and passively remain blind and indifferent, but you can't choose the consequences that will follow.

Ingratitude will take you where you don't want to go and keep you there longer than you want to stay, while charging you more than you want to pay.

Ingratitude fosters many maladies, from bitterness to suicide. And fasten your seatbelt for the following countercultural statement: thanklessness lurks behind homosexuality, envy, murder, and more.

A key text for understanding the outcomes of ingratitude is Romans 1:21–22: "Although they knew God, they did not honor him as God *or give thanks to him,* but they became futile in their thinking, and their foolish hearts were darkened. Claiming to be wise, they became fools."

Don't miss the structure of the argument: futile thinking and foolish hearts stem from ingratitude, from not honoring God for what he has done. Such ingratitude is the root of many other sins. Because ingratitude lies at the bottom of "all manner of unrighteousness" (Rom. 1:29), gratitude for God's truly good gifts is the right response in overcoming many sinful temptations and habits. For example, notice the word *instead* in this verse: "Let there be no filthiness nor foolish talk nor crude joking, which are out of place, but instead let there be thanksgiving" (Eph. 5:4).

When we insert wise thanksgiving, foolish talk will be on the run. Gratitude has the power to have that same effect on such things as boredom, unhealthy people-pleasing, peer dependency, and applause addiction.

WRONG EXPECTATIONS

One reason we find it unnatural and difficult to feel grateful when suffering is that we've tricked ourselves into a set of expectations that don't match God's. We think our expectations are perfectly understandable; that's why we have them. We think our expectations are perfect. Oh, we would never come right out and claim that we're always right, but at any given moment we *think* we're right. In fact, at *every* given moment we think we're right. If we discover we're wrong, we change our minds, and then once more think we're right. All of us do this, all the time.

Our expectations are warranted—so we think. Then when something doesn't go according to what we think God should have done, we get bent out of shape, perhaps angry, or sullen, or vengeful, or bitter, or suicidal, or gender dysphoric. Actually, we don't get bent out of shape; rather, we reveal the shape we're already in: namely, God-dismissing. The task before us is to yield our expectations to God and to his actual agenda flowing out of his infinite unassailable wisdom.

As novelist Ann Patchett says, "Never be so focused on what you're looking for that you overlook the thing that you actually find."[1] What we actually find is the perfect will of an infinitely wise God being relentlessly worked out for the good of those who love him. None of us live the life we would plan. We live the life God planned for us. Above our kitchen sink my wife has a small placard saying, "We plan. God laughs."

He is infinitely wise. We are not. We're wise to learn to be grateful when he sets aside our finite plans and works relentlessly for our good, even through adversity. We so easily miss the opportunity to revel in what God is doing, because we're looking

---

1   Ann Patchett, *State of Wonder* (San Francisco: HarperCollins, 2011), 246.

for something else. We identify with David and can say, "I am restless in my complaint and I moan" (Ps. 55:2). The grumbling heart says that God isn't treating me right. The grumbling heart claims greater wisdom and goodness than the infinitely wise God. Thanklessness huddles with complaint, and the two conspire to interfere with contentment, peace, and rest.

Practicing thankfulness for what's really happening all around us frees us from bondage to the slavery of continuously inventing "needs" that we trick ourselves into thinking we must have, picturing some version of life that we think we need but which falls short of the good plans God has for us through adversity.

It's crucial to recognize blessings in whatever form they come, and to recognize them as the blessings they are.

George Bailey, the main character in the classic film *It's a Wonderful Life*, despises his small town and his career, which he considers insignificant. He is about to commit suicide when an angel, Clarence, shows him what it would be like if George had lived none of the life he had lived. Once awakened to his blessings and standing in falling snow, George greets with jubilation the car he has crashed into a tree, greets the old building and loan office building with gladness, and enthusiastically wishes the town villain, Mr. Potter, a Merry Christmas. He suddenly loves his drafty old house and is tickled that he might get to go to jail on false charges of embezzlement. The secret to the change? He humbly prays, "Please, God." And his new awareness that he deserves none of the manifold blessings he has experienced over his lifetime usher him into utter jubilation. He does away with thinking he deserves any of it, and joy rushes in.

The doorway to joy is opened by putting to death a spirit of entitlement.

OUR WRONG SENSE OF RIGHTS

Ingratitude is rooted in our mistaken assumptions about our rights, our sense of entitlement.

Thinking always in terms of rights breeds demandingness. A spirit of entitlement expands and spreads so slyly, permeating the heart and mind. But under God we have no rights. All we have is privilege. He owes us nothing. Even our "right" to become children of God (as expressed in John 1:12) is actually a gift.

A spirit of entitlement and a spirit of demandingness are close neighbors. When I was a lad, my dad's employer announced to his employees they could all go home a half day early for Christmas Eve, with pay. Ready to lock up, Mr. Edsel held the door as staff zipped their coats and filed out to go home. My dad was the last one out and the only one to thank Mr. Edsel for the paid holiday, to which Mr. Edsel replied, "If that's all the appreciation people feel, then maybe that's the last time I'll do this."

Roger Mortimer wrote the following to his off-to-boarding-school son:

> Dear Charles, I have just had a letter from Aunty Joan asking whether you received a Christmas present from her. As in other matters of life, you are childishly idle about writing letters, thereby giving the impression that you are both ill-mannered and ungrateful. If people bother to give you a present, the least they can expect is that you rouse yourself

from your customary state of squalid inertia and write and say thank you. I am very fond of you but you do drive me around the bend.[2]

The term *deserve* is overused and abused in our day. The use of *deserve* is a plague on our culture, fostering worlds of selfishness and foolishness. We deserve what we've earned, which is the wage of our sin: death. All else is grace, for which a fitting response is gratefulness. The heart that thinks it deserves anything good from the hand of God displays its fallenness by thinking that way. Such thinking moves the individual in the opposite direction from gratefulness.

We read in Luke 17:12–19 about ten lepers who were healed by Jesus, but only one gave thanks to him for it. Where were the other nine? Did they think they had a right to be healed? Had they so soon forgotten that their benefit came from a benefactor?

THANKLESSNESS AS A SIN OF OMISSION

All a person has to do in order to be ungrateful is: nothing. Thanklessness can creep up on us. We might even be good thanksgiving theoreticians, while remaining poor practitioners. We've fallen asleep perhaps.

Perhaps we don't thank because we don't believe that what we've received is good, or enough, or thankworthy. Or we don't believe it came from the hand of God. Or we never take stock of blessings, but leave them "uncounted," taken for granted. And

2   Roger Mortimer and Charles Mortimer, *Dear Lupin: Letters to a Wayward Son* (New York: Thomas Dunne Books, 2011), 10.

before we know it, we become darkened in heart, like those Paul describes: "Although they knew God, they did not honor him as God or give thanks to him, but they became futile in their thinking, and their foolish hearts were darkened" (Rom. 1:21).

Being thankful involves counting. "Man only likes to count his troubles," wrote the Russian novelist Fyodor Dostoevsky, "but he does not count his joys."[3]

Not all thanklessness is conscious hostility or grumpiness. It can be simple neglect—preoccupation with other interests versus a mindset of active gratefulness. A mindset of entitlement can be conscious (as in holding up a placard on a sidewalk), or it can be passive and subconscious, as when I'm not even aware that I'm thinking I deserve some peace and quiet for my nap or that I deserve to have the line at the checkout counter move more quickly.

Nancy DeMoss Wolgemuth writes,

> If we take it all for granted, if we think life just shows up with this stuff already in place, if we trick ourselves into believing that everyday household items come from the grocery rather than from a gracious God, we walk right past countless reasons for worship [and, I would add, for giving thanks] without even knowing it.[4]

A mistaken sense of independence fosters ingratitude and hardens into a sense of entitlement and overweening pride and

3 Fyodor Dostoevsky, *Notes from Underground*, Project Gutenberg, part 2, chapter 6, posted September 13, 2008, http://www.gutenberg.org/ebooks/600/.
4 Nancy Leigh DeMoss, *Choosing Gratitude: Your Journey to Joy* (Chicago: Moody, 2009), 113.

presumption. Independence is a lie. None of us is independent. When we think we are, we earn the scriptural rebuke found in passages like this: "Do you thus repay the LORD, / you foolish and senseless people? / Is not he your father, who created you, / who made you and established you?" (Deut. 32:6).

A DANGER

In Romans 1:21, Paul says about mankind, "For although they knew God, they did not honor him as God *or give thanks to him*." They did not acknowledge him as the good giver of everything. And since they don't give thanks to him, what happens next? Paul tells us: "They became futile in their thinking, and their foolish hearts were darkened. Claiming to be wise, they became fools" (Rom. 1:21–22).

How is this dark foolishness exhibited? In idolatry, impurity, and dishonorable passion:

> They . . . exchanged the glory of the immortal God for images re-sembling mortal man and birds and animals and creeping things.
>
> Therefore God gave them up in the lusts of their hearts to impurity, to the dishonoring of their bodies among themselves, because they exchanged the truth about God for a lie and worshiped and served the creature rather than the Creator, who is blessed forever! Amen.
>
> For this reason God gave them up to dishonorable passions. For their women exchanged natural relations for those that are contrary to nature; and the men likewise gave up natural relations with women and were consumed with passion for one another, men committing shameless acts with men and receiving in themselves the due penalty for their error. (Rom. 1:22–27)

Again, where does all of that come from? It comes from thank-lessness. Sinfully debased minds result when we do not see fit to acknowledge God: "And since they did not see fit to acknowledge God, God gave them up to a debased mind to do what ought not to be done" (1:28).

Homosexuality isn't the only consequence of refusing to thank God. Paul lists much more:

> They were filled with all manner of unrighteousness, evil, covetousness, malice. They are full of envy, murder, strife, deceit, maliciousness. They are gossips, slanderers, haters of God, insolent, haughty, boastful, inventors of evil, disobedient to parents, foolish, faithless, heartless, ruthless. Though they know God's righteous decree that those who practice such things deserve to die, they not only do them but give approval to those who practice them. (1:29–32)

If homosexuality isn't the only consequence of thanklessness toward God, why do I single it out here? Why not highlight gossip or something else on the apostle Paul's list? I give homosexuality special focus because there has been so much discussion in the public square about the roots of homosexuality, with various advocates saying it's rooted in nature and others saying it's rooted in nurture.[5]

I do not disregard the potential helpfulness of the wide-ranging public discussion on homosexuality, but I'm inviting you to join

---

5 I'm well aware of arguments that draw a distinction between homosexual desire and homosexual behavior. I believe the Bible teaches that all homosexual arousal and desires are disordered and owing to sin in the world. They did not exist before the fall; they will not exist in the new heavens and earth. Paul connects ingratitude to homosexual behavior, which is rooted in homosexual desire, which in turn stems from thanklessness.

me in learning from Paul about what's at the bottom of all this. One might ask if we could have the same discussion about, let's say, gossip. Yes, gossip is also on Paul's list. But there isn't a massive discussion about gossip in the public square, with debates about whether it's caused by nature or nurture or something else, accompanied by Gossip Pride marches. So I've drawn our attention to a topic more widely debated. Further, in this list in Romans 1 Paul gives the most wordage to homosexual outcomes. Homosexuality is an outcome. I speak to the matter of homosexuality merely to show how vast and how deep are the consequences of not thanking God "always for everything."

You might exclaim, "Do you mean to tell me that a worldview-impacting lifestyle with decades of decisions and relationships flows out of a single root called thanklessness?" I would answer: Learn from the apostle Paul. Reread Romans 1:21–32, and watch for the flow of his argument. Don't miss words like *therefore* in verse 24, *because* in verse 25, and *since* in verse 28. I'm not saying thanklessness is the only thing going on with same-sex attraction, but without thankfulness you will get foolishness and futility, including sexual confusion.

Life is complex, and many forces are simultaneously at work, but thanklessness by itself is potent enough to pivot any person toward futility and foolishness.

6

THANKFULNESS IN ACTION

There's a profound difference between thankfulness as a concept and thankfulness as a practice.

People who think rightly about God's provision are thankful, and they *say* so. Thankers also feel. Thankers feel something because they're assuming something, thinking something, and concluding something. They may momentarily be fishing for words, but they sense something, *know* something—and their feelings line up behind the truth they're perceiving: that God is good, and his goodness feels good. Those feelings seek expression. They don't want to be corked up.

FEELINGS MATTER—AND SO DOES DOING

Feelings matter, but so does doing. To state the obvious, thanksgiving is an act of giving; it's an action. To practice thankfulness, you don't just feel something; you do something. Thanks is something you *give*.

The ten lepers healed by Jesus in Luke 17:12–19 felt something. They felt plenty—relief, shock, new empowerment. But nine of them did nothing about it. They didn't *do* thanking.

By not practicing thankfulness, they revealed something about themselves. And they robbed themselves. Only one of the ten acted on his sense of appreciation for what had been done for him, and thus enlarged his joy.

John Piper speaks of gratitude as "a feeling that arises uncoerced in the heart."[1] Is it *just* a feeling—something that could be induced by drugs? If a person becomes comatose or were hypothetically cryofrozen in suspended animation, how could we tell if he was grateful? We couldn't. In order for gratefulness to be evidenced as gratefulness, something must be displayed, some facial expression, some act, some speech. Hence the importance of *practicing* thankfulness.

Is thankfulness, then, only behavior—only a practice, without feeling? No. Otherwise an actor on a stage could carry out actions that correspond to thankfulness while not meaning them from the heart. A carefully programmed robot could perform the behaviors. Behavior isn't all there is to it. A grateful attitude isn't merely a choice or an emotionless transaction; it's a response of joy.

ENHANCED BY EXPRESSION

Being blessed is passive, not active. You can sit like a bump on a log and receive a blessing, but make no response. The whole world is blessed with common grace—sunrises, rain, refreshment, and countless other benefits. But the whole world doesn't respond with thankfulness. Thanking is active. It responds. It issues forth behaviors. In fact, it can't be stopped from doing so.

---

1 John Piper, "Grace, Gratitude, and the Glory of God," desiringGod.org, November 26, 1981, https://www.desiringgod.org/messages/grace-gratitude-and-the-glory-of-god/.

In a scene from a film adaptation of *Anne of Green Gables,* Matthew Cuthbert has given his foster daughter, Anne, a longed-for dress with puffed sleeves. She models it for Matthew's sister Marilla in the kitchen, twirling in delight. But before Anne can obey Marilla—who wants her to go upstairs and take it off before it gets soiled—she gleefully exclaims, "I have to thank Matthew." She runs off to the barn where he's doing chores. She *has* to. Grateful hearts *have* to say so, because they very much *want* to. If we aren't saying thanks, it says something about our thankless hearts. If Anne had greeted her new dress with only a shrug, or, "Well, it's about time!"—we would think something was profoundly wrong with that girl.

Speaking up can be a matter of serendipitous overflow in the moment; it can also be planned ahead of time. More on that later.

Thankfulness enjoys something, and thankfulness *expressed* enhances that joy. To be grateful and yet not express it is like learning a song but never singing it, riding to the top of the roller coaster but walking down, taking a deep breath but never exhaling, buying an ice cream cone but letting it melt and drip to the ground, getting a wedding ring but never putting it on. The gratefulness is completed and consummated in the expression of it.

Thankfulness is one of the ways joy signs its name. The *giving* of thanks springs from pleasure *and* produces more of it. It is not a random, vague, floating pleasure like drug-induced euphoria, but giving thanks helps complete or consummate the pleasure in the very provision for which you're grateful. Anne enjoys the dress even more because she expresses her overwhelming gratitude.

You've not quite maximized your pleasure until you express your appreciation. The expression of thanks is a component of the delight you receive from the blessing bestowed.

SERVING OTHERS

Because the giving of thanks is uplifting to those around you, your gratitude is an act of love toward them. Look upon your expressions of gratefulness as acts of love—toward God and toward others.

Furthermore, your expressions of thankfulness can make visible to others what, without your display of gratitude, might remain invisible to them. Your thankfulness may then be joined by thankfulness of their own. Giving thanks to people serves as a kind of reward for their service. Rewards increase the likelihood that such behaviors will be repeated.

THE COST OF GIVING THANKS

Expressing gratitude costs almost nothing. Anyone can do it, at any time. But it requires both the grace of God and our own obedient effort. Being genuinely grateful requires a work of God, a grace of wakefulness, a miraculous heart transformation. We are all born like puppies with our eyes closed, but God performs transformation. If gratefulness requires the appropriation of enabling grace in order to be able to give thanks, the good news is that there's also enabling grace for *appropriating* the enabling grace.

Appropriate (pronounced "uh-PRO-pree-ate"—it's a verb) grace. Consciously latch on to the enablement God gives you to do what you should do. Say to yourself and to God, "Yes, I will thank." There's no circumstance in which God's enablement for you will run short: "God is able to make *all* grace abound to you, so that having *all* contentment in *all* things at *all* times, you may abound in *every* good work" (2 Cor. 9:8).

There's never a day in which his grace runs out. His mercies are new every morning, and his enabling grace is abounding every night, sustaining you through the entire day every day.

Though enabling grace is available in endless supply, a grateful outlook doesn't just happen. It's not natural for self-preoccupied, rights-demanding, what's-in-it-for-me sinners. Beyond transformation and awakening, thankfulness requires cultivation. One of its dimensions to be cultivated is a biblical mindset. A heart that erupts with thanksgiving is a by-product of learning God's righteous judgments in the Scriptures: "I will praise you with an upright heart, / when I learn your righteous rules" (Ps. 119:7).

Though expressing thanksgiving costs almost nothing, *preparing* to give thanks—transforming the heart, cultivating the outlook, reading a book about the topic, being vigilant to spot opportunities to express gratitude—will cost something. It costs intentionality, desire, preparation, heart change, a stack of cards and envelopes, postage stamps, and time.

For example, we won't thank God for his mighty acts if we don't know them and remember them; therefore, the healthy practice of thankfulness hinges upon being people of the Book. The Bible records God's mighty acts in its history, and shows us how to recognize his mighty acts in our own lives.

GRATITUDE IS NOT A CHORE

Thankfulness is a response to pleasure or to anticipated pleasure (which is a kind of pleasure all its own). Thankfulness is feedback elicited by satisfaction. It's a fitting *re*action to a beneficial action. The soul encounters goodness, and voilà: it reverberates and erupts with joyful expressions.

Thankfulness is an expression of the heart's delight. Delight is not a burdensome chore. The grateful heart takes pleasure not only in the benefit but also in the benefactor. Note well that the grateful recipient understands that the benefactor was not obligated to provide the benefit; the provision was not owed to him. It's all grace, all unearned, all undeserved. The grateful heart sees itself as a have-not who has just received from a have. The grateful heart swims in an ocean of grace, breathes air of grace, stands on grace-ground, and expresses appreciation for the gift and the giver.

Though God receives our offerings, he isn't looking for our outward offerings that give back to him what he gave us in the first place. We arrived on the scene with nothing to bring to God, nothing with which to impress him. As Paul tells Timothy, "We brought nothing into the world, and we cannot take anything out of the world," which is why "godliness with contentment is great gain" (1 Tim. 6:6–7). Job expressed it this way: "Naked I came from my mother's womb, and naked shall I return. The LORD gave, and the LORD has taken away; blessed be the name of the LORD" (Job 1:21).

God is scanning us inwardly, looking for grateful hearts to accompany our offerings. He's looking for such hearts, and he *produces* such hearts. That's why we can speak of gratitude as being divinely given. (Remember again our working definition: *Gratitude is the divinely given spiritual ability to see grace, and the corresponding desire to affirm it and its giver as good.*)

Gratitude springs from the humility, brokenness, and contrition of heart that God does not despise (Ps. 51:17). Such heart-markers are always from him—and thus even more reason to be grateful.

7

THANKFULNESS AND
CONTENTMENT

Robert Louis Stevenson famously wrote,

> The world is so full of a number of things,
> I'm sure we should all be as happy as kings.[1]

But we're not as happy as kings. We're a race of complainers. Why? Here's one reason. Highly observant people can become critical people who then become unthankful people—complainers. Creative people are observant (and that includes those who are born again and are given eyes to see what they couldn't see before) and can see something. They see how something could be different, better. Seeing the possibilities prompts dissatisfaction with the status quo, and complaints can start tumbling out: That government office could surely shorten their waiting lines. That outfit worn by Aunt What's-Her-Name could have been

---

1   Robert Louis Stevenson, *A Child's Garden of Verses* (1885; Portland, ME: Thomas B. Mosher, 1899), 28.

more tasteful. That sermon could have been *way* better. All these observations might be true, but be on guard about becoming thankless regarding the government, the aunt, the sermon. People who can envision the most improvements can also become the most negative and critical.

Don't let that happen to you. Thank God for your powers of observation, and ask him to help you direct them in helpful, thankful ways.

If we refuse to be grateful now, we'll not likely be grateful if things change, because in this fallen world there will always be more room for improvement, an endless conveyor belt of things about which to complain.

CONTENTMENT VERSUS COMPLAINING

Instead of thinking the cup is half empty, the thankful heart is grateful that the cup is half full—and that there's even a cup at all. The complaining heart not only sees the cup as half empty but as too small in the first place—and the stuff in the cup isn't the stuff it wants.

The contented heart has enough. Sometimes the complaining heart has too much, and by doing without, the soul can discover appreciation for what was previously taken for granted or complained about. Solomon noted the productive benefits of deprivation: "A worker's appetite works for him" (Prov. 16:26).

Thankfulness isn't the only Christian virtue. It's not the final goal of Christian endeavor. Even though we're to be thankful for everything, including difficulties like illness, we work diligently to creatively eliminate these very problems.

Christians dig wells, build clinics, and teach literacy. The contentment that breeds thankfulness is not complacency. Christians thank God for problems, but that doesn't mean we don't seek solutions and thank God for those solutions when they come.

Every complaint is ultimately against the God who appointed everything that comes to pass, and every blessing is from God—no matter by what instrumentality it arrives. Thankfulness and contentment promote each other. Without them, your agitated heart will never have enough, never be at peace, and never mature. Notice what Paul associates with ingratitude:

> But understand this, that in the last days there will come times of difficulty. For people will be lovers of self, lovers of money, proud, arrogant, abusive, disobedient to their parents, *ungrateful*, unholy, heartless, unappeasable, slanderous, without self-control, brutal, not loving good, treacherous, reckless, swollen with conceit, lovers of pleasure rather than lovers of God, having the appearance of godliness, but denying its power. Avoid such people. (2 Tim. 3:1–5)

Avoid being such people. The thankless soul is dull, impoverished, and even perhaps dead.

NOT COMPLAINING, EVEN WHILE GROANING

Two things that don't coexist are whining and being grateful. One will consume attention required by the other.

God tells us, "Do all things without grumbling" (Phil. 2:14). Knowing this command, I became perplexed about how to live in a fallen world—with all its pain—yet without complaining. So I asked our counseling pastor at the time how to admit and acknowledge my suffering and the suffering of others, yet without complaining. He immediately took me to this verse: "For we know that the whole creation has been groaning together in the pains of childbirth until now" (Rom. 8:22).

If a woman is in the middle of giving birth, and you ask her, "How does it feel?" she's not going to wink and say, "No problem; what pain?" Instead, she might cry out in anguish. She's sweating and groaning and gasping for air. When it's all said and done, and she holds her newborn close, and you ask her if she would trade the child for a painless day, grateful mothers would not trade the baby. In fact, when the time is right, she might willingly go through all that pain again. That's the picture in Romans 8:22. What is being produced in us is worth the pain, so much so that we don't complain—*even when we groan.*

Joni Eareckson Tada has reason to complain. Having been paralyzed in a diving accident at age seventeen and living in a wheelchair for decades, she envisions herself some day in heaven thanking Jesus for her wheelchair:

> I hope I can take my wheelchair to heaven with me—I know that's not biblically correct, but if I were able, I would have my wheelchair up in heaven right next to me when God gives me my brand new, glorified body. And I will then turn to Jesus and say, "Lord, do you see that wheelchair right there? Well, you were right when you said that in this world we would have trouble, because that wheelchair was *a lot* of trouble! But Jesus, the weaker I was in that thing, the harder I leaned on you.

And the harder I leaned on *you*, the stronger I discovered you to be. So thank you for what you did in my life through that wheelchair. And now," I always say jokingly, "you can send that wheelchair to hell, if you want."[2]

She admits the misery, but instead of complaining she gives thanks.

There are benefits in having what we have, and in not having what we don't have and wouldn't want if we had it (mumps, mosquito bites, or 699 wives and 299 concubines—which weren't enough for Solomon, who thought he had to have more). The heart becomes disgruntled when it fails to actively find contentment in the benefits coming its way. The wise become self-aware about the impulse to complain, and when tempted to complain will instead give thanks.

The English hymn writer and theologian Isaac Watts described our tendency to complain as "disquietude of mind" and "peevish passions."[3] Thankfulness puts to rest the disquietude and unpeeves our peeves.

Consciously and intentionally "put off" complaining. I sometimes silently say to myself, "Shut up, Sam. Just shut up." Then I take the wretched thought I was about to express (no matter how legitimate it seems in the moment) and replace it with silence or with something true, honorable, just, pure, lovely, commendable, excellent, or worthy of praise (Phil. 4:8).

---

2 Joni Eareckson Tada, "The Holiest of Wheelchairs," Joni & Friends website, http://t.joni andfriends.org/radio/4-minute/holiest-wheelchairs/.

3 Isaac Watts, *The World to Come; or Discourses on the Joys or Sorrows of Departed Souls at Death* (London: Daniel Fenton, 1811), 339.

CONTENTMENT AND PEACE

Contentment is a command: "Keep your life free from love of money, and *be content with what you have*, for he has said, 'I will never leave you nor forsake you'" (Heb. 13:5).

Contentment requires an ability—an enabling grace again—to see above the dust and debris of this pedestrian earthly life. That ability or grace comes from God, who gives peace.

Paul instructed the Philippian Christians:

Let your reasonableness be known to everyone. The Lord is at hand; do not be anxious about anything, but in everything by prayer and supplication with thanksgiving let your requests be made known to God. And the peace of God, which surpasses all understanding, will guard your hearts and your minds in Christ Jesus.

Finally, brothers, whatever is true, whatever is honorable, whatever is just, whatever is pure, whatever is lovely, whatever is commendable, if there is any excellence, if there is anything worthy of praise, think about these things. What you have learned and received and heard and seen in me—practice these things, and the God of peace will be with you. (Phil. 4:5–9)

Note the flow of Paul's argument:

1. We want to end up with the God of peace being with us, governing our hearts, and granting us contentment.

2. That desired end, Paul tells us, results from *practicing* what we've received from Paul.

3. What we've received from him can be equated to what he describes as being true, honorable, just, pure, lovely, commendable, excellent, worthy of praise. Paul writes that believers are to

"think about these things"—to focus on them, to pay attention to them. These are obviously the kind of things for which we could and should be thankful.

4. This kind of thinking—about that which is noblest and best and most excellent—is made possible by hearts and minds that are *guarded* "in Christ Jesus." Guarded by what? By "the peace of God."

5. That peace comes about when we attack our specific anxieties by letting God know our specific prayer requests. And how are we to make such requests? "With *thanksgiving*." Thanksgiving is the antidote to peace-destroying anxiety.

6. Such grateful prayer is possible through our faith in the Lord's nearness—we know that he's "at hand." This faith and knowledge enable us to manifest "reasonableness" to those around us.

7. Because of this faith, again, we're enabled to demonstrate something to others around us—a certain "reasonableness" (or "graciousness" or "gentleness," as other versions translate it; the Greek word here has a wide range of connotations that include kindness, yieldedness, consideration, and leniency.)

Peace is at stake, depending upon whether we pray with *thanksgiving*. And a person's God-centered disposition—not one's circumstances—is what makes the decisive difference between misery or contentment. It's pivotal.

Our thankfulness is evidence of our peace and security—our confidence that God is working in our hearts to appreciate all that he has done. Thankfulness is evidence of being secured.

MORE THAN ENOUGH

Contentment concludes that what I have is enough. And gratitude transposes it into *more* than enough, making it a cause for celebration. As "clutter buster" Brooks Palmer playfully says, "The store was closed, so I went home and hugged what I own."[4] Contentment means realizing that God has supplied everything I need. Whatever I may have lost, there's always something left; what I need I still have.

In the next chapter we'll consider perhaps the highest pleasure of all.

---

4   Brooks Palmer, "The Store Was Closed, So I Went Home and Hugged What I Own," Clutter Busting website, August 15, 2009, https://clutterbusting.com/the-store-was-closed -so-i-went-home-and-hugged-what-i-own/.

8

THANKFULNESS AND WONDER

Consistently looking for opportunities to express gratefulness enlarges your capacity to see wonder, an especially valuable reward.

God's universe is jam-packed with benefits just waiting for us to see them as blessings. Those who are thus awake are continually startled with the wonders lying before their very eyes, sometimes under their literal noses and massaging their ears and taste buds. Other blessings are invisible, seen only by spiritually awakened eyes. Those who are awake are constantly grateful.

By learning to pay attention—to recognize the vast plenitude that already surrounds us—our alertness and attentiveness will fuel thankfulness, which in turn heightens more wakefulness in a wonderful and satisfying upward spiral.

Thus, gratefulness frees the grateful.

Seeing is one of the first steps to gratefulness. And gratefulness travels well with its cousin, cheerfulness: "The cheerful of heart has a continual feast" (Prov. 15:15). To be alert in this way means being vigilantly on the lookout for God's provision and blessings, thereby seeing the banquet that's all around us.

God has planted beauty in everything, but not everyone sees it. So-called normal days are coming down the tracks loaded with treasure, yet we're prone to miss the wonder because we're preoccupied by something else. As the poet David Whyte says, "Being unappreciative might mean we are simply not paying attention."[1] "Continue steadfastly in prayer, being watchful in it with thanksgiving" (Col. 4:2).

Remember our definition of gratitude from chapter 1? Gratitude is the divinely given spiritual ability to *see* grace, and the corresponding desire to affirm it and its giver as good.

ALERTNESS DEPENDS ON ALIVENESS

But something comes prior to that alertness. What is that requirement? We can observe it in the well-known story of the prodigal son (Luke 15:11–32).

What was the prodigal son's problem? I've asked over a thousand people that question, and their answers have included selfishness, immaturity, greed, narcissism, worldliness, carnal hedonism, peer dependency, stubborn rebellion, and more. All those answers are legitimate in some measure, but they're not the answer Jesus gives us in Luke 15—and he gives it twice. In the words of the father in that story, here's the son's problem: "For this my son was dead, and is alive again; he was lost, and is found" (Luke 15:24). The father repeats it in verse 32: "For this your brother was dead, and is alive; he was lost, and is found."

---

1 David Whyte, "Gratitude," in *Consolations: The Solace, Nourishment, and Underlying Meaning of Everyday Words* (Langley, Washington: Many Rivers Press, 2015), https://gratefulness.org/resource/gratitude-david-whyte/.

Because of his deadness, the son was thankless. His thanklessness toward the father was rooted in that deadness. While thankless, he was lost.

Likewise today, thanklessness in a person suggests that the person is dead toward God.

Prior to honing the kind of alertness that supports thankfulness, one must be alive. Jesus emphasized aliveness in his interaction with Nicodemus: "Nick, you're not alive. You must first be born! Unless you are alive, you cannot see!" (That's my paraphrase of John 3:3–5.) However, if by God's grace you are "appointed to eternal life" and thus believe and are made righteous by faith (Acts 13:48), you'll give thanks to his name. "Surely the righteous shall give thanks to your name" (Ps. 140:13).

Holy gratitude is fully awake and brimming with appreciation no matter the relative size of the blessing. The earnestness of genuine gratitude doesn't hinge upon calibrating and ranking the size of the blessing.

Once a person is alive in Christ (see Rom. 6:11; 1 Cor. 15:22; Eph. 2:5), he or she begins to cooperate with the Spirit in developing and imaging forth the character of Jesus, which includes qualities important to the practice of thankfulness. To grow in gratitude, one must (and will) develop such qualities as alertness, contentment, generosity, and humility.

In all of history, no one was more alert, contented, generous, and humble than Jesus, and when we demonstrate those qualities, we image forth his character. Many other qualities could also be named—cheerfulness (versus dourness), sensitivity (versus indifference), creativity (expressing thanks never before expressed), and more.

As for the matter of alertness, President Abraham Lincoln took strong criticism for signing the proclamation to establish a national day of thanksgiving, long petitioned for by the writer and editor Sarah Josepha Hale. Lincoln was accused of being vindictive and morally insensitive, because he called for thanksgiving during a time of war and national distress. It's not uncommon for those who give thanks during difficulty to be accused of being simpletons— Pollyanna ninnies too stupid to perceive the realities of difficulty surrounding them. But contrary to the allegation, a grateful heart is not *less* seeing, but *more* seeing than the complaining heart.

If expressing thankfulness serves to enlarge and complete the pleasure of enjoying God's sovereign grace and care for us, then ingratitude cheats the thankless. They rob themselves of soul-enlargement. The taste buds of a thankless heart aren't doing what they're designed to do—taste! The eyes of the thankless heart are blind to what it should be seeing: "Oh, taste and *see* that the LORD is good!" (Ps. 34:8).

Gratitude isn't only feelings, nor only thoughts, nor only behaviors. Deep down in the secrets of the heart, gratitude is a *valuing*, an appreciation for something or an aliveness toward someone, like the life hidden deep inside the cotyledon of the seed about to germinate.

Gratitude is thus a subcategory of a larger thing: worship. Thanksgiving is a form of exaltation, for it exalts the generosity of the giver. There are many ways to worship; thankfulness is one of them, one bulb in the marquee of worship, one pixel in the large screen of praise.

TO MARVEL AT THE MARVELOUS

Thankfulness greatly intensifies one of life's most precious capacities—namely, the capacity to marvel. We are created for it. We love to marvel. Marveling is perhaps our highest pleasure. Practicing thankfulness can enhance your perspective, and thereby make otherwise ordinary things sizzle with the extraordinary wonders God has hidden inside them. The extraordinary can be hiding just behind the ordinary, and in order to see it clearly, all you have to do is adjust the focal point of your lens. Seeing wonders, allowing them to pop with color and vitality in your heart and mind, and then expressing your sense of delight can enhance your own satisfaction and trigger the pleasure of those around you.

Most of us think of maggots as ugly, smelly, disease-ridden accomplices of death and decay, but even the maggot has a beauty and utility of its own. I admit to being startled (and a bit repulsed) when I watched a physician place a handful of living, squirming maggots on the open, infected leg-wound of his patient, and cover the teeming mess with a large bandage. Two days later he removed the bandage to find (as he expected) that the maggots, who are picky eaters, had crawled around inside the wound, cleaning it and accelerating the healing process which was being hindered by the dead flesh still in the wound. I marveled.

Some might call it being easily pleased to marvel at the ordinary. It might also be called being *rightly* pleased. In everything God designs and in everything he does, there's something of the marvelous. The universe serves God as a kind of silent instructor: "For his invisible attributes, namely, his eternal power and divine nature, have been clearly perceived, ever since the creation of the world, in the things that have been made" (Rom. 1:20).

Remembering again our privilege and responsibility to always thank God for everything, let's zoom in on that a bit closer.

Because everything is from him, thank him for the *specifics*. For example, at mealtime, instead of merely and generally thanking God for "this food," thank him for the Idaho potatoes, the creamy butter melted in the crevices, Romaine lettuce, snap peas, and the ice in the tea. Get specific. Instead of merely thanking him for health, thank him for kidneys that function, teeth that chew and aid speech, salivary glands that serve you all day long, and so on.

The delightful drill of exercising powers of observation with the aim of expressing gratitude even in the little things can show us that the little things may not be so dull after all. As Ray Bradbury puts it, "Stuff your eyes with wonder."[2]

Like the athlete building his muscles and endurance for next week's competition by exerting them in his workout today, expressing gratitude today opens up the possibility of developing an enlarged capacity for marveling tomorrow.

What makes something marvelous? Something marvelous is something that evokes emotion. Marvelous things elicit marveling.

Marveling is a spiritual activity. Rocks don't marvel. Living beings marvel, being stunned, astonished, impressed, wowed, astounded, awed. Marveling requires and displays an emotional capacity. To marvel is not only to experience an upward tick in adrenaline, but to have conscious thoughts join feelings and seek expression verbally. People caught up in marveling will do this aloud. They speak, even if only a comparatively speechless head-shaking "Hmm," which translated means, "Wow! Fantastic! Incredible! Would you get a load of that!"

---

2   Ray Bradbury, *Fahrenheit 451*, 60th anniversary ed. (New York: Simon & Schuster, 2013), 150.

Those who marvel speak. And one of the ways to speak is in song: "Oh sing to the LORD a new song, / for he has done marvelous things!" (Ps. 98:1)

I observe twin truths. First, the reason to sing is that there are marvels at which to marvel—chiefly salvation wrought by steadfast love and faithfulness. Second, a fitting way to marvel is to sing! The writer of Psalm 98 elaborates the marvels God has done:

> His right hand and his holy arm
>> have worked salvation for him.
> The LORD has made known his salvation;
>> he has revealed his righteousness in the sight of the
>>> nations.
> He has remembered his steadfast love and faithfulness
>> to the house of Israel.
> All the ends of the earth have seen
>> the salvation of our God. (Ps. 98:1–3)

God's marvels of deliverance and righteousness extend to "all the ends of the earth." Are you seeing them?

Admittedly, marvelousness is—in some measure—in the eye of the beholder. The capacity for marveling governs in some measure the marveling that will or won't erupt. One person is swept away with breathless tingling at the passionate stylings of Dvořák's *Cello Concerto* or Schumann's *Abendlied*, while another listener stops listening and dozes off or changes the channel in disinterested boredom.

In some degree, the capacity to appreciate lies within the appreciative. But it's not *only* in the eye of the beholder. As C. S. Lewis famously pointed out, children who are mesmerized by making mud pies when they could have a holiday at sea are misguided in their values and emotions.[3] They're immature, or blind, or dead. That is to say, there's an objective standard outside the human observer by which to gauge the marvelousness of something—namely, if it images forth the perfections of God himself.

Back to the earlier question: What makes something marvelous? What aspects make it marvel-*worthy*? Consider things like scale: How big, vast, fast, powerful is it? Things like scope: What else does it impact? Does it impact things down to their very core? Is it universal in its impact, influencing everything else? Or is it isolated and unattached? Does it convey grandeur? And consider this: Could you achieve it by yourself? If by yourself the accomplishment of something would be impossible (escaping an enemy, recovering from a deadly illness, salvaging a failing business, etc.), and help appears to be nowhere on the horizon but then suddenly arrives in abundance—that calls forth its own kind of marveling. Marveling with joy often erupts when help arrives at a point when all hope seems lost, especially when the help is massive, deep, and affects all else.

Sadly—tragically—powers of observation aren't so easily awakened. Sinners are born blind and dead. Earlier I said that marvelous things elicit marveling, but not necessarily. Absence of marveling may indicate dullness in the observer, not absence of spectacular aspects of the thing marvelous.

What sharpens one's ability to apprehend distinctions between the marvelous and the mundane? For one thing: contrast. Wise

3   C. S. Lewis, *The Weight of Glory* (San Francisco: HarperCollins, 2001), 25–26.

and jubilant marvelers distinguish. They do so by comparing and contrasting. When Lewis cites mud pies and holidays at sea in the same sentence, he's making a contrast, and he uses that contrast to send spiritual eyes in search of the truly marvelous.

To marvel, take care to note the difference between common and holy, ordinary and extraordinarily rare. (I think this is why Jesus marveled at the faith of the centurion with the ailing servant—it was a rare faith.) Discern the difference between what's vulgar and what's wholesome, or what's fitting and what's broken or despoiled. Learn to identify and be amazed at design versus happenstance, commonly overlooked complexity versus primitiveness, ingenious purposefulness versus seemingly random impulse, refined skill versus amateurishness. Paying attention to contrast can awaken the capacity to value the valuable. "Thank you" and "wow" are next-door neighbors.

9

THANKFULNESS AND SUFFERING

Let us not approach the subject of thankfulness thinking it will be all brightness and sweets and floral bouquets. Gratitude is a difficult doctrine, assuming things like the universal sovereignty of God, which encompasses sickness, sin, and even Satan. Thankfulness in trials is counterintuitive and begs for explanation.

A robust theology of suffering is essential. The person who cannot apprehend the good purposes of God in suffering and trust him to produce fruit through it, will not—cannot!—be thankful to him for it. And to refuse to be thankful, as we have seen, is to set the table for folly and futility.

In 1897, Johnson Oatman Jr. wrote the song "Count Your Blessings":

When upon life billows you are tempest tossed,
When you are discouraged, thinking all is lost,
Count your many blessings, name them one by one,
And it will surprise you what the Lord has done.

Count your blessings, name them one by one.
Count your blessings, see what God has done.

Observe that this song doesn't commend counting blessings only when the sun is shining after a good night's rest and the market is performing well for your 401(k). Rather, we recall our blessings when the tempest billows are tossing us about and we're discouraged, perhaps even thinking that all is lost.

Well, it isn't. All is not lost. It never is for the believer.

It took solid theological underpinnings to write a song like that—a healthy theology of suffering. When you're really sick, you need a healthy theology of suffering. When you're poor, you need a rich theology of adversity. In this fallen world, tempest billows will most assuredly toss. When it happens, we won't be thankful if we lack a biblical understanding of God's fruitful purposes in suffering. We'll instead pile up the spiritual debris that comes from thanklessness.

Prolong your meditation on the God who ordained these blessings you're counting. It's impossible to do a full accounting of all his goodness to us. Counting blessings can reorient disoriented hearts.

SUFFERING IS ALWAYS PRODUCTIVE FOR THOSE WHO LOVE GOD

What does it mean that God has fruitful purposes for our suffering? God doesn't waste one single moment of suffering. Suffering is *productive*. It's a means to an end. We glorify God by letting suffering produce what God designed it to produce.

My dad farmed. We had thousands of pigs on a small acreage, not enough acreage to handle all the manure. Fortunately, our neighbors coveted the manure for their land. The process of spreading that manure wasn't at all appealing. Its smell was pungent and offensive. What are farmers thinking when spreading excrement all over their valuable cropland? Answer: crops. They are thinking of what it will produce. They are thinking future. In the same way that unsavory manure produces savory crops, unsavory adversity and tragedy is productive, producing the good fruit God is aiming to produce in our lives. We can view painful tragedies through the forward-looking eyes of faith.

Here are three texts to support the purposeful fruit-producing of suffering:

> We rejoice in our sufferings, knowing that suffering produces endurance, and endurance produces character, and character produces hope, and hope does not put us to shame, because God's love has been poured into our hearts through the Holy Spirit who has been given to us. (Rom. 5:3–5)

> Count it all joy, my brothers, when you meet trials of various kinds, for you know that the testing of your faith produces steadfastness. And let steadfastness have its full effect, that you may be perfect and complete, lacking in nothing. (James 1:2–4)

> So we do not lose heart. Though our outer self is wasting away, our inner self is being renewed day by day. For this light momentary affliction is preparing for us an eternal weight of glory beyond all comparison, as we look not to the things that are seen but to the things that are unseen. For the things that are seen are transient, but the things that are unseen are eternal. (2 Cor. 4:16–18)

How valuable is the fruit that God will produce through our suffering? Paul says that suffering produces "an eternal weight of glory far beyond all comparison." It's so valuable that it can't be compared with anything else. Later in Romans, Paul confirms this again: "For I consider that the sufferings of this present time are not worth comparing with the glory that is to be revealed to us" (Rom. 8:18).

For believers, affliction is always temporary, and it never ends in destruction but in fruit. People who don't believe this will not retain God in their thoughts or give thanks to him. And when they fail to give thanks, foolishness and futility are on the way.

In the book of Genesis, Joseph remains merciful toward his conniving brothers, who meant his slavery as harm. He remains merciful because he believes that God meant their actions for good: "As for you, you meant evil against me, but God meant it for good" (Gen. 50:20).

Again, God gives us *everything*: "He himself gives to all mankind life and breath and everything" (Acts 17:25). And that includes unsavory and painful things:

- *Calamity.* God declares, "I form light and create darkness; / I make well-being and create calamity; / I am the LORD, who does all these things" (Isa. 45:7); "Who can speak and have it happen / if the Lord has not decreed it? / Is it not from the mouth of the Most High / that both calamities and good things come?" (Lam. 3:37–38 NIV).
- *Deafness, blindness, muteness.* "Then the LORD said to him, 'Who has made man's mouth? Who makes him mute, or deaf, or seeing, or blind? Is it not I, the LORD?'" (Ex. 4:11).
- *Adversity.* "But he said to her, 'You speak as one of the foolish women would speak. Shall we receive good from God and

shall we not receive evil?' In all this Job did not sin with his lips" (Job 2:10).

- *Affliction.* "Make us glad for as many days as you have afflicted us, / and for as many years as we have seen evil" (Ps. 90:15).
- *Famine.* "When he summoned a famine on the land / and broke all supply of bread, / he had sent a man ahead of them, / Joseph, who was sold as a slave" (Ps. 105:16–17).

This is not an exhaustive list. God himself designs these difficult things, yet without being himself evil. The wise and grace-enabled soul will trust that God is working *all* things for the good of those who love him (like sending Joseph ahead via slavery). That kind of healthy soul gives thanks to God for all things, knowing God is always working flawless good in everything, even in our difficulties that seem the worst. When the famine comes, God is not done; he is rescuing all of Joseph's people *through* the famine.

We know, for example, that adversity develops character, and that strong character is needed in order to face the world with maturity and confidence. It takes confidence in an all-wise God to be grateful in ugly situations. To handle ugly situations beautifully is already a beauty by itself, and the beauty of gratefulness for small things opens up powers of observation for endless other things—and I do mean endless.

The thankful person therefore always has a faith-filled, steady context in which he can process bad news. "He is not afraid of bad news; / his heart is firm, trusting in the LORD. / His heart is steady; / he will not be afraid . . ." (Ps. 112:7–8). Thankfulness helps us overcome fear, depression, anger, outrage, bitterness, suicide, and more. Think of it this way: A person cannot simply tell himself, "Don't be depressed." It doesn't work. You can't just decide to not be depressed. But a person *can* decide to give thanks. And the giving of thanks works against depression. And fear. And anger. By directly practicing thankfulness, the person indirectly fights his depression or fear or other negative sentiment.

Remember again that God's instructions are to thank him always and for everything. Even mosquitoes are God's idea, appointed to assist us in the development of our Christlikeness. Aside from the fact that they're pollinators and play a role in the food chain (many game fish eat mosquito larvae, and Jesus ate fish just like we do), mosquitoes humble us, reminding us that we're not always in charge and that we don't understand all of God's purposes. He's not obligated to explain himself to us, and that humble admission on our part is healthy for us. So thank God even for mosquitoes.

SHOULD WE NOT TRY TO END SUFFERING?

Just because God ordains suffering and produces fruit through it doesn't mean we become masochists or sadists. We don't just throw up our hands and passively say, "Que sera sera." We labor to end as much suffering as we can. But in a fallen world, some suffering will be inescapable. We strive to cure diseases, build bridges that won't collapse, provide for sanitation, and invent useful products and services. Only an overstriding eschatology presumes we can end all suffering, all hunger, all conflict, here and now. This isn't heaven. Not yet. When heaven arrives, God's timing for making all things new will be found to have been impeccable.

HYPOCRITICAL THANKFULNESS?

When you're experiencing the genuine hurt of physical or emotional suffering, you may think that trying to be thankful would only be hypocritical, since you certainly don't feel grateful.

It's true that Jesus spoke strongly against hypocrisy. He labeled the Pharisees as hypocrites, whose insides were like whitewashed tombs full of rotting cadavers, and he said our righteousness must exceed their outward righteousness. But consider that a hypocrite who from an imperfect heart expresses gratefulness that rightfully ought to be expressed is better than a genuine demon who doesn't express any. This is no justification for hypocrisy. But the hypocrite who *wants* to be grateful even before *feeling* grateful is on the way to expelling the hypocrisy lurking in his heart.

Genuine gratefulness sometimes starts out as contrived and insincere. For example, we've noted that we can't just stop being depressed by telling ourselves to not be depressed. However, by realizing that thankfulness counteracts depression, we're motivated to find things for which to give thanks. Because depression makes us feel lousy, and we don't want to feel lousy, the relief we can anticipate from practicing gratitude provides us with an incentive to get busy giving thanks, thereby minimizing the misery of the blahs, and setting the table for us to eventually feel better, feel grateful.

When you feel thankless, acquiring actual feelings of gratitude can feel far beyond you, totally out of reach. First, repent. Ingratitude is wrong, so admit the wrongfulness of a thankless heart. Second, ask God for renewed gratefulness in the heart. Third, obediently begin thanking (chap. 12 may help you). Do all this in anticipation that God may grant you genuinely earnest, heartfelt gratitude. That kind of anticipation is another word for *faith*.

The act of giving thanks can spark growth in heartfelt gratefulness. Such enlarged hearts of gratitude will seek expression in more giving of thanks, and so it will cycle upward in the strength God supplies.

Job famously said, "Though he slay me, yet will I trust in him" (Job 13:15 KJV). In the midst of terrible circumstances, we can honor God long before we feel like doing so, and we can pray that while we're obeying him, our feelings will wake up and catch up.

"Give thanks" is a command, so we should get on with it. Then we should seek to grow in thoughts and feelings that align with the goodness of God in our circumstances. It's like a child learning to floss his teeth or eat his broccoli or wash behind his ears. At first he doesn't feel like doing any of it, but as he matures, he does such things when no one's asking or looking. He has internalized the command. Ask God to incline your heart to do the same.

SUFFERING AND OUR LOVE FOR GOD

We often fail to experience gratitude in the midst of adversity because we don't see all of God's purposes in the moment. We might accept that it's good to give thanks to God when the crisis is over—but in the *middle* of suffering?

By faith, however, we're enabled to genuinely thank him for suffering and *in* suffering—thanking him that he's working all things *right now* for the good of those who love him. Our troubles may prevent for now the comfort and contentment we long for, but we can know and trust that these adversities will bring greater comfort and contentment later.

So thank swiftly. As Walter Russell Bowie prayed, "Teach us to . . . be swift to speak the grateful and happy word."[1]

Does everything turn out well in the end for both believer and unbeliever alike? No, not in the end. When we understand Romans 8:28, we aren't thanking the adverse situation itself. Instead, we're thanking the infinitely wise God who wastes nothing and who is working the difficulty for the good of those who love him. Have you seen and understood the condition that's stated in Romans 8:28? God works all things together for the good of *those who love him.* So even when we're suffering, the key question is: Do you love God? Even in the midst of God-appointed suffering, we can love the God who appointed the suffering when we have confidence that he's using it to produce a weight of glory for us far beyond all comparison. I can love the dentist who drills my teeth. I can love the coach who requires me to run another batch of hill sprints when my lungs are already about to burst. They labor for my good, and the pain I experience is the very route I must take in order to get the good I want.

MY PERSONAL ADVERSITY

You may be thinking, Sam, you speak of thanking God for adversity and suffering, but have you personally ever suffered much? That's a fair question. Let me mention a couple varieties of pain I've suffered, not as a badge of honor, but to assure you I'm not speaking hypocritically from an insulated ivory tower of ease.

---

1   Horton Davies, ed., *The Communion of Saints: Prayers of the Famous* (Grand Rapids, MI: Eerdmans, 1990), 131.

I've suffered physical pain, including multiple broken bones. On one occasion I received two broken ribs and a broken finger when I was struck by a car while biking. That meant pain even just in breathing, and for three weeks I couldn't lie down and I didn't dare sneeze or cough. Years earlier I endured hernia surgery with its disabling postoperative dysfunction and impediments to motion. A decade ago I developed blood clots in both lungs, with excruciating pain, so that I could barely breathe for several days. The doctor approached my hospital bed and asked, "Are your affairs in order? Is your will up to date?" Then he leaned in and asked, "Do you want us to resuscitate?" Apparently, I was in trouble. I know I was in intense pain and without sleep for days.

I've also suffered emotional trauma. Thieves have broken in on multiple occasions, rifling through everything, on one occasion ripping copper plumbing out of the house. I've been wounded by betrayal. Part of my forgiveness of those who wounded me by betrayal is that I don't go into detail about it, but it was a life-altering wound.

I've lost two children.

Here's the main point in sharing these things: I don't ever want to go through these kinds of suffering again, and yet some of the greatest benefits in my life have been delivered to me through precisely such adversity. I wouldn't wish the pain on anyone I love, but it was worth it because of the fruit such pain is producing in my life. In the wise hand of God, our greatest suffering is producing our greatest growth, fulfillment, satisfaction, and eventual delight.

Over the years I've asked many individuals if, looking back, they would say that the gains that came to them through the darkest chapters of their lives gave them cause to thank God. They unhesitatingly join me in saying yes. Admittedly, it's more difficult to say yes while you're still in the middle of the shock and hurt, but in that moment, God is not finished. He supplies strength to hang in there. Give thanks by faith.

THANKFULNESS AND TEARS

So often it seems humanly impossible to hold misery and gratitude close at the same time. It's tricky and requires enabling grace. But there *is* grace for it, and the Bible teaches it. Like Paul, we can view ourselves as being "sorrowful, yet always rejoicing" (2 Cor. 6:10). We can be thankful even in our tears.

I knew my mother, Adele Rose Joop Crabtree Cross, for six decades. Most people say commendable things about their mothers, and it's proper that they should do so, but my mother was exceptional. I'm aware that some might think I honor my mother here simply because she was mine, but all who knew my mother would attest that she was a remarkably winsome woman who was exceptionally winsome in her Christian faith.

Years before she died, I anticipated that I of course would grieve her passing, and I wondered what that grieving would be like. When I was twenty-seven, at my dad's funeral, tears had run down my face and dripped off my chin, but I suspected that grieving for my mom would be different. After all, I knew her more than twice as long, since she outlived my dad by more than three decades. She loved the grandchildren my dad never met.

When she died, I spoke at her funeral. My emotions were brimming, but I didn't experience the kind of deep grieving I'd expected.

A few weeks after her passing, I was leading a staff retreat at a conference center. I was up before sunrise reading my Bible and journaling, when suddenly I began to cry—to *sob*—so loudly that I feared I would awaken the sleeper in the next room. As I wept, I was mainly experiencing amazement at the privilege that was mine to have such a mother. I was mainly grateful, not grim.

I wasn't feeling ripped off, but privileged. Who am I to have enjoyed six decades of such remarkable grace in my life? Was there loss? Of course. But I was sensing mainly thanksgiving—profound and sweet gratefulness that God had appointed this boy to have such a mother. Tears and thankfulness mingled—they were not incompatible.

Paul states that we as believers grieve, but not as those who have no hope (1 Thess. 4:13). Grief and gratitude need not be polar opposites. They can team up in pointing to the beauty of what is transient. Today my mother is more beautiful than ever, though I can't see her. But I could see her transient momentary life, even seeing it *better* through grief with thanksgiving.

THE CRUCIAL PIVOT POINT

A crucial pivot point in every heart is whether we grasp and embrace this truth: *God is producing something through our suffering.* He is producing something in us, and he is producing something through us for others. To not embrace this is to look away from him, to not give him thanks—yes, even for the pain—and to become foolish and heart-darkened as he gives us over to confusion, to false paradigms, and to dark lusts of our hearts.

Failure to embrace the sovereignty of God in suffering brings tragic results. If we don't believe God is producing worthwhile fruit in our suffering, we won't thank him. And if we won't thank him, he will give us over to the foolish futility we inadvertently prefer.

But well-intentioned people who sincerely desire to be grateful persons sometimes fail to be. What's getting in the way?

10

HINDRANCES TO THANKFULNESS

If reasons to thank God are all around us, and if we're convinced that good things are produced by giving thanks, and if we also know that thanklessness will produce rotten fruit and regrettable consequences in our lives, then what hinders us from giving thanks? What's stopping us?

Inertia, for one thing. From the day we're born, we whine and fuss, and by the time we reach adulthood we're already well-practiced in the arts of self-focused ingratitude and complaining. We're a race of natural-born ingrates.

For another thing, we see ingratitude modeled all around us. Others are griping, so we join the chorus. So many others fail to be thankful, so why shouldn't we? Plus there's so much we could complain about. We live in a broken world. We're preoccupied with making a living, raising the kids, and making the wheels go around that we fail to focus on the giving of thanks. Busy, busy, busy—we can so easily miss the opportunities to express gratefulness that are floating past all around us.

But there's an even stickier impediment to giving thanks. The most serious hindrance to gratefulness is our chronic spiritual blindness.

Moses speaks about our not seeing what's looking us in the face:

And Moses summoned all Israel and said to them: "You have seen all that the LORD did before your eyes in the land of Egypt, to Pharaoh and to all his servants and to all his land, the great trials that your eyes saw, the signs, and those great wonders. But to this day the LORD has not given you a heart to understand or eyes to see or ears to hear." (Deut. 29:2–4)

Seeing without seeing. As blessings come our way, sometimes we're so blinded that we see only the benefits, but never the benefactor. Or we fail to see the blessings as blessings, and see them instead as inconveniences, annoyances, or curses. True sight sees rightly: "As we look not to the things that are seen but to the things that are unseen. For the things that are seen are transient, but the things that are unseen are eternal" (2 Cor. 4:18).

Even when we see the transient, we may miss the eternal. We can easily see the wasting away of the outer self, but then we fail to see the inner self being renewed.

Jesus refers to the same dynamic of seeing without seeing:

"For this people's heart has grown dull,
and with their ears they can barely hear,
and their eyes they have closed,
lest they should see with their eyes
and hear with their ears

and understand with their heart
and turn, and I would heal them."

But blessed are your eyes, for they see, and your ears, for they hear. (Matt. 13:15–16)

Do I have eyes that are open to really see? Bill Hull writes,

For people to catch a vision, they must first open their eyes. Spiritual realities are not easy to perceive, especially when one has spent an entire lifetime wearing spiritual blinders. Jesus said, "I have come into the world . . . so that the blind will see" (John 9:39).[1]

Jason Meyer writes about our struggle to see rightly:

The problem is that we are blind to his glory. The god of this age has put a blindfold over our eyes so that we cannot see the glory of Christ on the cross (2 Cor. 4:3–4). Conversion is a new creation work of God that overcomes our spiritual blindness and darkness.

Seeing the cross with these new eyes decisively defeats pride. Why? Those who see the cross rightly see themselves rightly. We see him on the cross and we see our sin. The cross reveals what we deserve from God. We cannot receive the grace of Christ apart from seeing and embracing the undeserved disgrace of Christ.

There is not sightless sanctification. We're transformed from one degree of glory to the next by beholding the glory of the Lord (2 Cor. 3:18). So sanctification is a struggle to see rightly.[2]

---

1   Bill Hull, *Jesus Christ, Disciplemaker* (Grand Rapids, MI: Baker, 1984), 24.
2   Jason Meyer, "Pride," in *Killjoys: The Seven Deadly Sins*, ed. Marshall Segal (Minneapolis: Desiring God, 2015), 14–15.

Consider also these lines from the poet Elizabeth Barrett Browning:

Earth's crammed with heaven,
And every common bush afire with God:
But only he who sees, takes off his shoes,
The rest sit round it, and pluck blackberries.[3]

Some of this blindness is a product of our own making. We blind ourselves by sinning. Iniquity is blinding. As David writes, "My iniquities have overtaken me, / and I cannot see" (Ps. 40:12). Here, it's not that blindness produces iniquity; it's the other way around. Stubborn sinfulness inflicts the sinner with an inability to apprehend. It's no good for him to try to be watchful, for he cannot observe much less recognize. If he's headed straight for a ditch, he's oblivious. In his fog, he cannot see if a bridge is out.

Iniquity has the power to overtake. Iniquity is not benign or inert, but active. It doesn't lay there like a passive shadow. Rather it goes places, produces effects, brings lesser powers into captivity. In Psalm 40 the loser is "me"— I am the one with the iniquities. There's no finger-pointing at others.

But the profoundly good news for us all in Psalm 40 is that the one who has been blinded by his own iniquities is beginning to see. He sees his blindness! He's awakening to his bondage. His spiritual eyes are being restored. Sight is given to the blind. God is being merciful. Every saved sinner can sing "I was blind, but now I see."

---

3   Elizabeth Barrett Browning, *Aurora Leigh*, book 7 (1856). This epic poem is part of the University of Pennsylvania's digital library, https://digital.library.upenn.edu/women /barrett/aurora/aurora.html.

As God gives you grace in overcoming blindness, remember: everyone is an instrument in his hand. So make a conscious effort to *see* people, and then thank them: children, spouse, pastor, laity, neighbor, clerk at the store . . . yes, even the telemarketer.

Thankfully, gratefulness is a habit that can be cultivated. Ask God to enable you to become radically grateful from the heart. And ask him, again and again, to open your eyes.

11

VARIOUS QUESTIONS ABOUT THANKFULNESS

Writing a book is a good way to discover how much you don't know about something. I make no claim to having mastered the practice of thankfulness. Questions and problems beg for answers. This chapter is an effort to address some of them.

WHAT SHOULD I DO ABOUT MY PET PEEVES?

It depends on what they are. Perhaps you're an easily peeved person. Thank God for the peeve, and grow up. Grow out of it. Yield your expectation that you're the center of the universe, that things ought to go according to your preferences, that everyone will read your mind and do what you prefer. It bothers you that the home team keeps losing ball games? Adjust your expectations. Die to them. You didn't think children would spill, or the traffic would be slow, or the weather would be inclement? Change your expectations. If you embrace the likelihood that children will spill, traffic will barely creep, and your parade will get rained on, you'll take things more in stride.

Meanwhile, if your peeves are legitimate grievances, seek to fix them and remove the irritation. Keep tripping over that rug? Do something about it. Don't like the way you keep stubbing your toe on that piece of furniture? Move it. Instead of cursing the darkness, light a candle.

Or, make an appeal. Don't like that neighborhood pothole? Contact the street department.

Meanwhile, thank the sovereign God who appointed this peevish circumstance for your good and your refinement, to mobilize you to invent a solution, and to use the peeve to deepen your desire for heaven.

SOMEONE CLOSE TO ME JUST SUFFERED A MAJOR TRAGEDY. HOW SHOULD WE PRACTICE THANKFULNESS IN THIS SITUATION?

Apply compassionate sensitivity. Just because we're to give thanks always for everything doesn't mean that thanksgiving is the first thing that comes out of our mouths at such a time. Be present with them. Groan with them. Enter into the sorrow with tenderness. Hugs and tears do not remove thankfulness from the situation, but set the table for being "sorrowful, yet always rejoicing" (2 Cor. 6:10). When the time is right, the Spirit will guide you into what to say.

Your loved ones are experiencing hostile terrorist persecution? Groan. Intercede. Advocate for them. And keep in full view the sovereignty of a good and great God who is not done.

WHAT SHOULD I DO ABOUT PROBLEMS IN MY CHURCH?

Thank God for the problems. Let them cause you to lean on him. Pray. It's not your church. Pray to the one whose church it is.

Meanwhile, make sure your facts are right. Be ready to acknowledge you might be wrong, even in some small measure, in how you view these problems. Whatever appeal you make, make it courteously, making charitable judgments. Do good to all, even before the problem is addressed or fixed. Be ready to forbear. You may not be able to fix the problem or transform the persons involved. Remember that when there's more than one opinion, you may not get your way. Others may prevail. God is still working it all for the good of those who love him.

Read Romans 2:1 slowly, and be prepared for the possibility that the problem is located in you: "Therefore you have no excuse, O man, every one of you who judges. For in passing judgment on another you condemn yourself, because *you, the judge, practice the very same things.*"

WHAT SHOULD I DO ABOUT FRUSTRATING WEAKNESSES IN THE PASTOR?

Thank God for the imperfect leadership God has appointed in your life. All pastors have weaknesses. Remember that your pastor has an imperfect flock. Ask yourself what you think he should do about frustrating weaknesses in his people.

Admit your own weaknesses (get the log out of your own eye). Pray for him. Encourage him. Always commend what's commendable. If and when the time is right, humbly offer a good suggestion.

WHAT ABOUT IRRITATING FLAWS IN MY SPOUSE?

Thank God for joining you to your husband or wife. Remember that our great bridegroom, Jesus, has a bride who is now far from perfect, even adulterous and idolatrous, and yet in demonstrating his own extremely attractive beauty he maintains fidelity to his covenant toward her. He does this even in the face of excruciating treatment he voluntarily suffers from her and for her.

Follow this progression:

1. Can Jesus love an imperfect bride (the collective members of his body)? Yes.
2. Can Jesus love an imperfect individual? Yes.
3. Can a wise, courageous, and Spirit-filled spouse love an imperfect sinful spouse? Yes.
4. With God's help, can *you* love an imperfect spouse? Yes (at least theoretically).
5. So then, will you?

The flaws in your spouse (or children, or parents, or coworkers, or boss, etc.) may be precisely the flaws God knows will be required to refine your own Christlikeness. A. W. Pink reminds us that our "disappointments are His appointments."[1]

WHAT SHOULD I DO ABOUT POOR QUALITY SERVICE FROM A VENDOR OR LANDLORD?

Thank God for the opportunity to grow in Christlikeness. Respectfully bring the problem to the attention of the party whose responsibility it is. Work through authorities. If possible, offer to be part of the solution.

---

1 Arthur W. Pink, *A. W. Pink's Studies in the Scriptures, 1928–1929* (Lafayette, IN: Sovereign Grace, 2001), 4:183.

SHOULD WE TEACH CHILDREN TO SAY THANK YOU WHEN THEIR HEARTS AREN'T TRULY APPRECIATIVE?

Heartfelt expressions of gratitude are courteous. Meanwhile, there's also courtesy in expressing thanks even before the heart is fully persuaded. That's one reason why it's good to teach children to say thank you long before it becomes spontaneous. Pray that the heart will catch up with the courtesy conveyed.

Teach them the appropriately grateful words, and teach them also the appropriateness of the context (saying thank you is good manners). Commend them when they do say thank you, and especially when their heart seems truly thankful. Pray that their hearts would genuinely grow in gratitude, erupting in unsolicited expressions of thanks as they grow and develop.

SHOULD I SAY THANK YOU FOR THE UGLY SWEATER I RECEIVED FOR CHRISTMAS?

Always thank *God* for all things. That doesn't mean you should speak falsehood about things that are ugly. If it's ugly, you would be lying to call it beautiful. But truth-telling is also to be accompanied by things like kindness and discretion. So first thank God for the sweater, the donor, and the opportunity for you to grow in Christlike character. Then thank the donor for things that you can honestly be grateful for: his generosity, his thoughtfulness in giving a warm sweater in a cold season, and so on.

If you pause long enough to ask God to help you think of legitimate positives, you'll get creative in observing what you may have overlooked. Then mention those things.

Meanwhile, just because something is true doesn't mean you're required to say everything about it. You don't have to say that your aunt is fat, your uncle is too boisterous, or the sweater they gave you is ugly. Many true things can be left unspoken without lying about them.

SHOULD I WRITE THANK-YOU NOTES FOR THE THANK-YOU NOTES I RECEIVE?

Ordinarily, while being grateful for expressions of gratitude that come our way, it's not customary to write thank-you notes in response to people's thank-you notes to you. (I recommend John Piper's excellent treatment of this kind of "debtor's ethic" in his 2008 sermon "Is Gratitude a Bad Motivation for Obeying God?"[2]) You can simply be grateful to God for the kind note you received. You don't have to get drawn in to an endless cycle of sending thank yous for thank yous.

2 John Piper, "Is Gratitude a Bad Motivation for Obeying God?," desiringGod.org, July 9, 2008, https://www.desiringgod.org/interviews/is-gratitude-a-bad-motivation-for-obeying -god.

12

ONE HUNDRED WAYS
TO BE THANKFUL

Why do we need suggestions on how to express gratitude? Shouldn't a truly grateful heart just naturally overflow in expressing that gratefulness, without needing to be prompted by tips? Well, yes. But recall that while the Bible speaks of acts of love bubbling over from transformed and loving hearts, it nevertheless gives us lots of instruction in *how* love might behave, including exhortations and commands to do it this way or that. Similarly, the truly grateful heart may be increasingly open to counsel on how to go about showing thankfulness. To such a heart, suggestions don't feel like a burden. Or like law.

Think of the young man in love with a woman. He wants to show love to her by showering her with gifts. So what does he do? He asks her sisters and roommates and mom what his heartthrob likes so that he can proceed to do those things for her. He wants suggestions!

Since gratitude isn't merely a doctrine to learn but a spiritual mindset to experience, below are a hundred "starters" for the heart hungry for ideas on how to demonstrate gratitude. Each of the following suggestions is easily made God-centered. For example, when thanking the pastor for a good sermon, you can say something like "I thank God for your faithful preaching," or some expression that places God in the center of the good being performed by that preacher.

1. In the checkout line, when retrieving my credit card from the credit card reader, I pretend the little screen says, "Be sure to thank helpful and intelligent [name of employee]," and so I "read" it out loud. Invariably I get a happy reaction from the store associate as well as from customers within earshot. Why not be energy-giving to public servants who experience their share of cranks?

2. My church provides a worship folder or bulletin. I routinely jot notes to myself on it as the service moves along, reminding me to thank people such as the pastor for his faithful and timely word, or the musicians for their practice and execution, or the ushers for alertly welcoming newcomers, or the folks who keep the coffee urns refilled, and so on.

3. During holidays, thank people for decorating. Decorations make a difference, don't they? Thank the decorators for making a difference.

4. Thank people for gifts you receive from them.

5. Express thanks up and down the chain of command—thank your supervisor, those you oversee, and your peers. (While there's a proactive aspect of leadership—initiating action and pulling the team forward—there's also a vitally important reactive aspect. In a job I held for fifteen years, I was responsible for more than 250 employees on the pay-

ONE HUNDRED WAYS TO BE THANKFUL

roll. I invested significant time and attention thanking and commending people for what they were doing. It's good for morale, it highlights what's valued, and it rewards good behaviors and patterns. Behaviors rewarded tend to recur.)

6. Say aloud, "I don't want to take [the act, the person] for granted." Then act.

7. Write your city's mayor, thanking him or her for public service in general, or for a specific action.

8. Thank God for something specific you've never thanked him for before. (I try to make this a regular practice.) A subcellular component, a body part, a product on the market, a relative's middle name, an element, a promise, a verse, a word—get specific.

9. When saying a table grace before a meal, with open eyes look at the food items and thank God for them specifically and by name—the potatoes with skins, the asparagus tips, the tomatoes that went into the French dressing, and so on.

10. Contact a civic leader and thank him or her for something specific—the recent pothole repairs, the training for the police officers, or the new street sign.

11. Ask God to make you increasingly grateful. Ask him now— before moving on to the next tip.

12. Write a prayer that is only thanks and praise—no requests.

13. Say to your children or grandchildren, "I want to be a thankful person. Tell me, who do you think I should thank for something?" Ask them to be specific. Then follow through.

14. The next time you go to church, be on the lookout for someone to thank for something.

15. Identify one of your pet peeves. Then identify something good God produces through it. Thank him for the peeve and the fruit in your life that comes from it.

16. Thank God for including in the Bible the story of Jesus healing the ten lepers. Reread it.

17. Write a fictional short story told either through the eyes of the one grateful leper or through the eyes of one of the other (ungrateful) lepers.

18. Thank God for preserving the Bible for you from centuries of banning, burning, and abridging.

19. Name the most painful experience in your life, whether the pain was physical or emotional. Then read passages such as James 1:2–4, Romans 5:3–5, or 2 Corinthians 4:17–18. Thank God for the productivity in your life that he's accomplishing through the pain you've experienced.

20. Express your gratefulness for how Jesus endured such deep suffering.

21. Thank God that he uses all things to conform you to the image of his Son (Rom. 8:28–29). Specifically think of one of the most difficult things he has allowed in your life. Thank God for how he has used that difficulty to help you become more like Jesus in some specific way (such as gentleness, endurance, compassion, courage, or wisdom.)

22. Write a new verse to a Thanksgiving hymn.

23. The next time you encounter a police officer, thank him or her for routinely facing dangerous situations in order to preserve your safety. If you encounter law enforcement officers at a gas station or convenience store or similar place, offer to buy them coffee.

24. Stock up on thank-you note cards and envelopes. Don't put them all away; keep at least one of them out to immediately write and send a thank-you.

25. Thank God for someone you've never met—perhaps someone who brought the gospel to your part of the world, or the lab technician who helped develop the drug in your prescription, or the assembly line worker who assembled your car, or the sanitation department worker who processes the sewage from your home, or the editor who proofread this book before it was published.

26. Thank God for an invention you may have taken for granted—door hinges, paper, circuit breakers, staples, Velcro, or adhesive tape. Then thank God for the inventor.

27. Are you satisfied with a consumer product? Let the manufacturer know. (Companies are more likely to hear from disgruntled customers than satisfied customers.) Brighten their day.

28. At the restaurant, don't just leave a tip for the table server. Speak your appreciation to him or her and perhaps to the management.

29. When spotting workers cleaning public restrooms, or picking up litter in or near a store, or emptying the garbage receptacles at the park, thank them for keeping the place shipshape.

30. Start early to plan a short speech of gratitude for your family gathering at Thanksgiving. Perhaps thank God for something unique about each family member.

31. Thank God for "common graces," the provisions he gives alike to all people: the sunrise, rain, air, chirping songbirds,

the passing of the seasons, tides that circulate the oceans, gravity, and so on.

32. Thank God for "particular graces," which he gives only to believers: election, predestination to justification, calling, regeneration, propitiation, adoption, repentance, sanctification, and glorification.

33. Read Ephesians 2:8, then thank God for your faith.

34. Thank God that you have face recognition and can recognize your friends. (Neuroscientists have identified something called "face blindness," which renders its victims unable to distinguish one face from another. The afflicted are unable to recognize their parents, spouses, children, or anyone.) Then thank God for specific friends by name. Thank him for childhood friends you can recall.

35. When I walk to our downtown Minneapolis office, I walk past the residence of a man with crippled legs; on one of his feet, he wears a shoe with a sole perhaps eight inches thick. He walks with a profound limp and sway. Never in his life has he run. Thank God for your feet and legs, and for the privilege of feeling the wind in your face when running. Thank God for shoes. Thank God for the beautiful feet that brought you good news (Isa. 52:7).

36. Thank God for your eyes that can read. Read about the wondrous complexity of your eyes, and thank God for each part of your eye and its wonderful function.

37. When one of my grandsons was born, he was in intensive care for several days. When Caleb had dampened his diaper, I volunteered to change it. While his mother and I navigated the tubes and wires to change the diaper, he

began to do something the doctors had been waiting for. He passed his very first bowel movement—meconium. Tears ran down my face. I was joyful, for it was evidence that everything was working after all. Thank God for the wondrous "routine" operation of your bowels, without which you would die.

38. Put this book down and look around to identify something specific nearby. Then look more closely at it. Thank God for the details related to something right in front of you right now. (In my case, I look up and I see a wooden cupboard door. Looking more closely I see wood grain. Back when the board was a tree, sap was coursing through that wood grain—more in the summer, less in the winter. That tree stood outdoors naked for years and decades, sometimes through subzero winters, sometimes through blistering hot summer spells. God sustained it, and now I have a cupboard door. He superintended every aspect of it: winters, summers, rains, roots, photosynthesis, sunlight, carbon—all of it.)

39. Make a list of favorite things—chocolate, donuts, Tchaikovsky's Symphony no. 4, your dog—and take delight in thanking God for them.

40. I receive numerous update letters from missionaries around the world. I often scribble comments on them and mail them back, so that we're having a conversation. I'm especially grateful for photographs they include, so I say so. Consider what expressions of thankfulness you might extend to a missionary, and to God for that missionary.

41. When eating fruit, think of the person who planted the tree, or picked the fruit, or boxed it, or shipped it.

42. Take a lined sheet of paper and write the letters of the alphabet vertically down the left margin. Then list things that begin with each letter of the alphabet and thank God for each of them. This is a simple exercise to do with children.

43. Thank God for something you benefit from that didn't exist at the time you were born.

44. Thank God for something that no longer exists (Alexander the Great's empire, the cross of Jesus, the Mayflower, etc.).

45. Learn how to say thank you in a handful of other languages. Then put it to use in conversations.

46. What if the world were black and white and gray? Thank God for colors. Thank him for the cones in the retina of your eyes that let you see these colors.

47. Thank God for a bad habit he has enabled you to overcome.

48. Thank God for a good habit he has established in your life.

49. Thank an influencer in your life who helped you address a habit—a coach who helped you with your swing of the bat at the plate, a physician who helped you quit smoking, a mentor who encouraged your pattern of Bible reading, a counselor who helped you improve your relationships or self-acceptance, and so on.

50. Look at one of your body parts, and thank God for it. Look more closely—perhaps with a magnifying glass—and thank God for the component parts. What lies beneath the skin? Thank God for those parts too. Thank God for things like digestion, respiration, and circulation that keep that body part alive and functioning.

51. Meditate on these words of David: "I will give to the LORD the thanks due to his righteousness, / and I will sing praise

to the name of the LORD, the Most High" (Ps. 7:17). Sing a song that gives thanks to God. Invite someone to sing it with you.

52. Name an aroma for which you're grateful.

53. Thank God for a place, a location—a room, building, city, island, or planet.

54. Go for a walk and find a dozen things to thank God for.

55. Thank someone you've never before thanked.

56. Memorize Psalm 100. Find at least seven things in those five short verses to thank God for.

57. Write a note to the pastor of a church other than your own, thanking him for his partnership in the great gospel cause.

58. Ask God to make gratitude not merely a task you do, but a way of life, a way of seeing, a way of valuing.

59. Set a timer and practice one minute of silence, if you can. Thank God for the experience.

60. Thank the Father (John 14:26) and Jesus (John 15:26) for sending the Holy Spirit. Explain what difference it makes to you that he was sent.

61. The Holy Spirit is called the Helper. Thank him for some specific help he has given.

62. List things money cannot buy. Give thanks to God and others for them.

63. Name a biblical promise God has made. Thank him for that promise.

64. The most common way to convey thankfulness is to say it. Think of the body parts used to express thankfulness—mouth, tongue, teeth, lips, lungs, and voice box. Thank God for designing these organs, knitting them together

in your mother's womb, and giving them to you at no charge—so that you can *say* thank you.

65. Have you received a compliment from someone? Say thank you to that person. And thank God for giving you the wherewithal to do what you're being complimented for. Invite the person who complimented you to join you in giving thanks to God.

66. Write a note of appreciation to your pastor's wife, thanking her for her contribution to his effectiveness.

67. At work did you receive a raise? A holiday? Don't take it for granted. Say thanks.

68. Do something nice anonymously for someone. Since it's anonymous, he or she won't be able to thank you. Let that absence of gratitude to you intensify the humble gratefulness in your own heart toward God who has given you a zillion things for which you haven't thanked him.

69. As part of eating at a restaurant, consider accompanying your generous tip with words of appreciation for such things as alertness (refilling your glass), cheerfulness in serving you, and so on.

70. Does your voicemail have an opening greeting? Is there anything in there that sounds grateful?

71. Conduct an "open mic" time when individuals can come to the mic and fill in the blank: "I thank God for _____." Or, how about a "thankful wall" at work? Or a whiteboard in your classroom?

72. Do you use a study Bible? If so, write a thank you note to the publisher or to any of the contributors who wrote the study notes.

73. The passage of time can numb our appreciation for profoundly significant events. Pause and reflect upon the fundamental impact in your life that was unleashed by such distant past events as which egg and which sperm combined to produce you, or which childhood diseases you survived. Remember also that in the distant past, Jesus had you in mind when he went to the cross. Repel complacency, let the significance of such events wash over you, and give thanks.

74. Identify someone to thank specifically for mercy—the bank teller who forgave that overdraft fee, your spouse who forgave you and kept on loving you even after you used that tone of voice for the zillionth time, or the creditor who accepted your late payment without penalty.

75. Think of an ordinary task you do that a very young child cannot do—tie a shoe, shine your shoes, boil water, use scissors, throw a spiral football pass, or unsnag a sweater. Thank the people who taught you these things. If they're deceased or unreachable, thank God for them.

76. Thank family members for something associated with each room of the house—thank them for hanging up their coats in the entry, for putting their bicycles away in the garage, for doing another load of laundry, for organizing the stuff in the trunk in the attic, for putting the dishes in the dishwasher, for hanging up towels, for putting socks in the hamper, for shoveling the walks, and so on.

77. Thank God for the courage and faithfulness of a specific Christian martyr by name. If you can't think of any, consult resources such as *Foxe's Book of Martyrs* or the website of Voice of the Martyrs.

78. Do you know someone who's consistently grateful? (Don't hurry past this question; pause until you come up with a name.) Thank that person for his or her good example.

79. To express my thanks, I wrote to previous pastors who led churches I attended down through the years, starting in my boyhood. (Some are deceased, so I wrote to their widows.) I also contacted previous high school and college teachers I hadn't seen for decades. Every response from them was warm. Who helped you years or decades ago? A Sunday school teacher? Your first employer? Let them know you still think of them to this very day with gratitude.

80. Take a photo every day of something you are thankful to God for. Make a gallery.

81. When attending a funeral or reading an obituary or scanning the year-end editions of magazines such as *Time* and *World*, which publish the notables who died that year, thank God by name for people who lived commendable lives and provided us with examples of how to live. Thank him also for those who gave us examples of how *not* to live.

82. Do you have a favorite book of the Bible or a favorite verse? Thank God for that specific writer by name, and for the circumstances that led to the writing of that passage.

83. Reflect on these opening words from Psalm 75: "We give thanks to you, O God; /we give thanks, for your name is near" (75:1). Notice that word *for.* It points to the basis, the reason for giving thanks. What should we do when God's name is near? *Give thanks.* Plunder the riches of the Bible, looking for reasons for giving thanks. And then— give thanks.

84. Pray a prayer of confession admitting thanklessness. Then thank God for forgiveness and cleansing.

85. Stand in front of a cupboard or drawer or closet and thank God for each and every item in there.

86. Find a copy of the hymn "For the Beauty of the Earth" and sing each verse. Thank God for Folliot S. Pierpoint, who wrote the lyrics.

87. Thank God for your biological sex, which he knit together for you in your mother's womb (Ps. 139:13–14). Thank God for your mother's womb.

88. Send a thank-you note to someone who expressed Godward words of comfort during a time when you were struggling—words that seemed to be a personal touch of Jesus in your life.

89. Pray for the author of this book and this list. Ask God to enable him to not be a hypocrite by talking about gratefulness while so often being whiny, complaining, and grumpy.

90. God used key individuals as instruments in leading you to faith in him. Thank him for the individuals who led *those* people to the Lord.

91. Think about these words from G. K. Chesterton and apply them to your life: "You say grace before meals. All right. But I say grace before the concert and the opera, and grace before the play and pantomime, and grace before I open a book, and grace before sketching, painting, swimming, fencing, boxing, walking, playing, dancing, and grace before I dip the pen in the ink."[1]

---

1 G. K. Chesterton, "A Grace," in *The Collected Works of G. K. Chesterton* (San Francisco: Ignatius Press, 2012), 10:43.

92. Look at your hands and fingers. Marvel that God gave them to you. Think of all the tasks you've accomplished with them, and thank him. Thank God for your mother's hands. Or your dad's.

93. Our responsibilities and obligations can often feel more like burdens than blessings. But these are privileges, when seen through grateful eyes. Everything from paying taxes to changing the baby's diaper can be a privilege when you think of the services purchased by the taxes, or of the babies whose digestive systems don't work properly, and so on. List some of your responsibilities and thank God that he has given them to you to carry out for his glory.

94. You breathe about twenty-three thousand times per day. Don't take it for granted. To paraphrase Psalm 150:6, let everything that has breath give thanks—thanks for that breath and for everything else.

95. Sing "Count Your Blessings" after reading the lyrics thoughtfully.

96. Count your blessings, and *do* name them one by one.

97. Has a piece of music ever elicited your tears or made you tap your toes with upbeat enjoyment? Marvel at this, and give thanks that God designed a world in which catgut or wire (for violin strings) can be strapped to a wooden box (violin or fiddle), and then rubbed with horse hairs (of all things!) fastened to a rod (the bow), and that those vibrating strings can then jiggle the molecules in the air until the vibrations reach your ear, where they're transferred through wax and a thin drumlike membrane and three tiny bones, onward to the intricate cochlear nerve up to the brain,

where—voilà—you hear it as toe-tapping "Oh! Suzanna" or the mournful romantic second movement of a Tchaikovsky violin concerto. Amazing! God invented the whole auditory apparatus that makes that happen. Thank him that he designed the universe and your body and soul to operate in these ways. Thank him for the whole material universe that makes music possible, and thank him for individual component parts.

98. Look through your wallet, and allow the contents to trigger expressions of gratitude. Thank God for such things as the date of your birth, your health insurance, your ability to drive a motor vehicle, and so on.

99. Send a letter to Crossway, thanking them for the kinds of books they publish.

100. Add your own suggestion to this list, and thank God for the creativity to do so.

ACKNOWLEDGED WITH THANKS

One day Peter Olney walked into the small group that meets in our home. While taking off his coat, he said, "I know the next book you should write: *Practicing Thankfulness*." He gave his rationale, I took him seriously, and you hold it in your hands.

Dave DeWit at Crossway injected his encouragement from the get-go.

Nancy DeMoss Wolgemuth added, "I hope you'll write the book Crossway is proposing—in my opinion, *there can't be too many books on gratitude*, and we can't be reminded too often of the need for this grace."

Thomas Womack contributed his structural editing eye.

Years ago God gave me Vicki Gail, and she was so gracious and supportive as I gave days "off" and vacation time to this project.

Years before that, Miss Crain taught a five-year-old boy to read in Bureau Junction, and oh, how grateful I am!

All these and more are instruments in the Redeemer's hand, and I just became aware that in front of my keyboard with elbows propped up on the desk, hands together so that fingertips on opposite hands are lightly touching and index fingers slowly tapping my lips, I am repeatedly whispering, "Thank you, Lord. Thank you, Lord." Yes.

GENERAL INDEX

adultery, 112
adversity, 92–93, 97–99
affliction, 49, 92, 93
American Psychological Association, 45
Anderson, Paul, 40–41
anger, 94
Animism, 33
Anne of Green Gables (film), 65
anonymity, 124
anxiety, 77
appreciation, 17, 48
appropriating, of grace, 66–67
aroma, 123
astrology, 33
atheism, 31–32, 33

beauty, 80, 93, 100
behavior, 64
Bible, 126
Bishop, Cindy Lubar, 28
bitterness, 53, 54, 94
blessings, 24, 57, 64, 81, 89–90, 104, 128
blindness, 92, 104–7
Bloom, Jon, 43
boredom, 53, 85
Botton, Alain de, 46
Bowie, Walter Russell, 97
Bradbury, Ray, 84
breathing, 23–24, 38
brokenness, 69, 103
Browning, Elizabeth Barrett, 106
Buddhism, 20, 33

calamity, 92
character, 93
cheerfulness, 79, 81
Chesterton, G. K., 27, 31, 127
children, 113
Christian life, 38
church, 110–11, 116, 117, 126
Cicero, 44
civic leaders, 117
collapsed bridges, 21
Collins, Gary, 46
commands, 96, 115
common grace, 34, 64, 119–20
compassion, 118
complacency, 73
complaining, 71–75
completion, 30
compliments, 124
confession, 127
consequences, of gratitude, 12
contentment, 55, 71–78, 96
contrast, 86–87
cost, of thankfulness, 66–67
courage, 118
covetousness, 51
creativity, 81
Cross, Adele Rose Joop Crabtree, 99
cultists, 33

Daniel, 38
David, 27, 106, 122–23
deafness, 92
debts, 31
delight, 68, 98

demandingness, 56
demons, 19
dependence, 39–41
depression, 94, 95
deprivation, 72
destructiveness, 52–53
deserve, 57
"disquietude of mind," 75
Dostoevsky, Fyodor, 58
Dvorak, 85

Eickstadt, Paul, 22
emotions, 86
endurance, 118
entitlement, 56, 58
envy, 44, 51, 53
eschatology, 94
existence, 17
expectations, 53–56

face blindness, 120
faith, 21, 24, 77, 96
falsehood, 113
famine, 93
farming, 90–91
favorite things, 121
feelings, 31, 63–64, 84
flaws, 111–12
folly, 12
foolishness, 53, 57, 59, 61
forgiveness, 98
Foxe's Book of Martyrs, 125
fruit, 91
fulfillment, 98
futility, 61

gender dysphoria, 54
generosity, 18
gentleness, 118
God
    access to, 38
    goodness of, 13, 18–19, 22
    love for, 96–97
    love of, 49
    promises of, 123
    providence of, 33
    sovereignty of, 25, 89, 110
    wisdom of, 54–55

godless positivity, 46
gossip, 60–61
grace, 17, 18, 66–67, 120
Graham, Billy, 37
gratitude
    as active, 64–65
    consequences of, 12
    and contentment, 71–78
    cost of, 66–67
    definition of, 11–12, 18, 68, 80
    in everything, 20–21
    fruitfulness of, 43–49
    as genuine, 35
    goodness of, 24
    hindrances to, 103–7
    wisdom of, 27–34
greed, 80
grief, 99–100
groaning, 73–75, 110
growth, 98
grumpiness, 58

habits, 122
Hale, Sarah Josepha, 82
happiness, 45–46
heart
    as grateful, 68–69
    hardness of, 46–47, 58
hedonism, 80
Heidelberg Catechism, 33
hindrances, to thankfulness, 103–7
Hitler, Adolf, 11
Holy Spirit
    cooperation with, 81
    as Helper, 123
    in our hearts, 45
homosexuality, 51, 53, 60–61
hope, 25, 29, 48, 100
Hull, Bill, 105
humility, 28, 39–41, 69
hypocrisy, 95–96

idolatry, 18, 51, 59, 112
immaturity, 11, 80
improvements, 72
indebtedness, 31
independence, 58–59
indifference, 36

ingratitude, 12, 23, 51–61, 95, 103
iniquity, 106
irrationalism, 34
It's a Wonderful Life (film), 55

jealousy, 44
Jesus Christ
    aliveness of, 81
    and centurion, 87
    giving thanks, 39
    as paying the price, 16
    on seeing, 104–5
    submission to the Father, 28
    suffering of, 118
    transformation by, 36–39
Job, 96
Joseph, 92, 93
joy, 19, 48–49, 55, 64, 65, 86
judgment, 111

law enforcement officers, 118
Lazarus, 39
Lewis, C. S., 85–87
Lincoln, Abraham, 82
Little, David, 25n3
Longman, Tremper, 19
luck, 29–30, 34

maggots, 83
manure, 90–91
marriage, 111–12
marvel, 82–87, 128–29
maturity, 11, 52
mealtime, 44, 84, 117
mental health, 46
mercy, 125
Meyer, Jason, 105
missionaries, 121
Mohler, Al, 11–12
morale, 46, 48
Mortimer, Roger, 56–57
Moses, 49, 104
mosquitoes, 21, 30, 75, 94
murder, 51, 53
Murray, Andrew, 45
music, 128–29
muteness, 92

Napoleon, 11
narcissism, 80

neglect, 58
neutrality, 52
Nicodemus, 81

Oatman, Johnson, Jr., 89–90
observation, 86
omission, sin of, 57–59
ordinary things, 20, 83, 87
outrage, 94

pain, 74, 98
Palmer, Brooks, 78
"particular graces," 120
pastors, 126
Patchett, Ann, 54
Paul
    on completion, 30
    on goodness of God, 18
    on grief, 100
    on hardness of heart, 58
    on homosexuality, 61
    on ingratitude, 73
    on mankind, 59
    on peace, 76
    on receiving, 17
    on repentance, 46–47
    on salvation, 16
    on suffering, 91–92
    on thankfulness, 44
peace, 46, 55, 76–77
persecution, 37
perseverance, 48
pet peeves, 109–10, 118
petitions, 25
Pierpoint, Folliot S., 127
Pink, A. W., 112
Piper, John, 18, 64, 114
pivot point, 11–13, 47, 100–101
pleasure, 65–66, 67
police, 118
praise, 82
prayer, 45, 77, 117, 127
preaching, 116
pride, 36, 58
privilege, 120, 128
psychology, 45–46
pushing, 31

ransom, 15–16
rationality, 29
rebellion, 80
regret, 12, 13
relationships, 52
repentance, 46–47, 95
rest, 55

sacrifice, 40
salvation, 16, 27
same-sex attraction, 61
sanctification, 105
Satan, 89
satisfaction, 49, 68, 98
Schumann, Robert, 85
secularists, 32–33
seeing, 79, 104–7
selfishness, 57, 80
self-righteousness, 44
sensitivity, 81
sermons, 72, 116
serving, 66
sickness, 33, 89, 90
silence, 75
sin
    doctrine of, 89
    homosexuality as, 60n5
    of omission, 57–59
    revealed on the cross, 105
Solomon, 72, 75
specifics, 84
Sproul, R. C., 29–30
Stevenson, Robert Lewis, 71

strength, 41
suffering, 49, 74, 89–101
suicide, 53, 54, 94

Tada, Joni Eareckson, 74–75
Tchaikovsky, Pyotr Ilyich, 121, 129
tears, 99–100
thankfulness. See gratitude
Thanksgiving (United States), 32–34, 82, 119
thank-you notes, 35, 114, 119, 124, 127
theology, of suffering, 90
thinking, 27–31
time, 125
tipping, 119, 124
transformation, 36–39, 66–67, 115
Trinity, 28, 123
truth-telling, 113–14

ugly situations, 93
understanding, 28
universe, 29, 30, 43, 83, 129

values, 86

Watts, Isaac, 75
weakness, 111
Western culture, 20
Whyte, David, 80
wisdom, 12, 27–34, 118
Wolgemuth, Nancy DeMoss, 58
wonder, 79–87
work, 24
worldliness, 80
worship, 82

SCRIPTURE INDEX

Genesis
3:15–19 51
50:20 92

Exodus
4:11 92

Deuteronomy
29:2–4 104
32:6 59

Job
1:21 68
2:10 93
13:15 96

Psalms
7:17 123
34:8 82
40 106
40:12 106
51:17 69
55:2 55
56:12–13 27
75 126
75:1 . . . . 34, 126
90:14 49
90:15 . . . . 49, 93
92:1 24
92:12 7
92:14 7
97:12 48
98:1 85
98:1–3 85
100 123

100:4 38
105:16–17 93
112:7–8 93
119:7 67
139:13–14 127
140:13 81
150:6 128

Proverbs
15:15 . . . . 46, 79
16:24 48
16:26 72
30:18–19 20

Isaiah
45:7 92
52:7 120

Lamentations
3:37–38 92

Daniel
2:23 38

Matthew
11:25 28
13:15–16 105
20:28 16
26:27 39

Luke
10:21 . . . . 28, 39
15 80
15:11–32 80
15:24 80

15:32 80
17:12–19 . . . . . . 57, 63
22:17–19 39

John
1:3 28
1:12 56
3:3–5 81
3:16 24
9:39 105
11:41 28
11:41–42 39
14:26 123
15:26 123

Acts
13:48 81
17:25 . . . . 17, 23, 32, 92

Romans
1 . . . . 29, 61
1–2 47
1:18 34
1:20 . . . . 51, 83
1:21 . . . . 58, 59
1:21–22 . . . . 53, 59
1:21–32 . . . . 51, 61
1:22–27 59
1:24 61
1:25 61
1:28 . . . . 60, 61
1:29 53
1:29–32 60

2:1 111
2:4 47
5:3–5 . . . . 91, 118
6:11 81
8:7 37
8:18 92
8:22 74
8:28 . . . . 18, 97
8:28–29 118
8:32 17
11:36 37

1 Corinthians
4:7 17
15:22 81

2 Corinthians
3:18 105
4:3–4 105
4:16–18 91
4:17 19
4:17–18 118
4:18 104

6:10 . . . . 99, 110
9:8 67

Ephesians
2:5 81
2:8 120
2:8–9 24
5 21
5:4 53
5:20 . . . . 20, 21

Philippians
1:6 30
2:14 73
4:5–9 76
4:8 75

Colossians
1:16–17 28
2:6–7 36
2:7 37
3:16–17 36
4:2 . . . . 45, 80

1 Thessalonians
3:9 48
4:13 100
5:18 . . . . 20, 21, 36

1 Timothy
1:12–15 16
4:3–5 44
6:6–7 68

2 Timothy
3:1–5 73

Hebrews
13:5 76

James
1:2–4 . . . . 91, 118

Revelation
11:16–19 38

Also Available
from Sam Crabtree

"When it comes to affirming and encouraging others, some people come by it naturally. For the Christian, we come by it supernaturally. However, even the most mature believer must hone and cultivate the act of affirmation—that's why this book by Sam Crabtree is such an invaluable resource to the church. How do we effectively 'build each other up in the faith?' You're holding the answer in your hands!"

JONI EARECKSON TADA, Founder, Joni and Friends
International Disability Center

For more information, visit **crossway.org**.